Sioux
Code Talkers
of World War II

Sioux
Code Talkers
of World War II

Andrea M. Page

PELICAN PUBLISHING COMPANY
Gretna 2017

First printing, February 2017
Second printing, April 2017

*The word "Pelican" and the depiction of a pelican are
trademarks of Pelican Publishing Company, Inc., and are
registered in the U.S. Patent and Trademark Office.*

Library of Congress Cataloging-in-Publication Data

Names: Page, Andrea M., author.
Title: Sioux code talkers of World War II / Andrea M. Page.
Description: Gretna, LA : Pelican Publishing Company, [2017] | Includes
  bibliographical references and index. | Audience: Grades 4-6.
Identifiers: LCCN 2016026431| ISBN 9781455622436 (hardcover : alk. paper) |
  ISBN 9781455622443 (e-book)
Subjects: LCSH: World War, 1939-1945—Cryptography—Juvenile literature. |
  Indian code talkers—Juvenile literature. | Dakota Indians—Juvenile
  literature. | World War, 1939-1945—Participation, Indian—Juvenile
  literature. | United States—Armed Forces—Indians—Juvenile literature. |
  Indians of North America—History—20th century—Juvenile literature.
Classification: LCC D810.C88 P34 2016 | DDC 940.54/8673—dc23 LC record
  available at https://lccn.loc.gov/2016026431

Printed in the United States of America

Published by Pelican Publishing Company, Inc.
1000 Burmaster Street, Gretna, Louisiana 70053

For John Bear King, the Sioux Code Talkers, and the members of the 302nd Reconnaissance Troop, who served our country with honor.

For my uncle Claude Black Cloud, who enlisted in the army during the Vietnam War and is a role model for bravery, fortitude, generosity, and wisdom.

For my family members who serve(d) our country, including my brother, Jerry Monsees, and more than sixteen cousins, nieces, nephews, uncles, and an aunt from the Black Cloud/Monsees and Munn/Page families.

For John "Jack" Gibbons Langan, who inspired me to persevere and explore the unknown.

For my parents, Walter and Mary Monsees, who always believed in me and never let me give up.

Contents

Preface

Mitakuye Oyasin
—Lakota greeting meaning "all are my relations"

I grew up with rules. Of course these included the usual rules of chores, cooperating with my siblings, and trying my best at school. But one main rule was drilled into our heads as children more than any other: respect your elders. I didn't grasp the entire concept of this type of relationship with my elders until adulthood. I was always courteous and caring around my aunts, uncles, and grandparents, but I learned the most profound lesson of respecting my elders in 1994, when I began researching the military service of my great-uncle John Bear King. I am forever changed and deeply honored to be connected to the elders in my *tiyospaye* ("family community"), my ancestors, and my friends who have shared this journey with me. This book is a culmination of my research of the Lakota Code Talkers' service in the First Cavalry Division during World War II.

I was never fascinated by history while growing up in Rochester, New York. When I was young, I struggled to communicate through writing. I was very shy and afraid to share my thoughts. In fact, it wasn't until college that I had a suitemate sit down with me and teach me proper writing techniques. My sentence structure was all mixed up. I realize now that I struggled because English was a second language for both of my parents.

My mother was born and raised on the Standing Rock Sioux Reservation in South Dakota, and my father was born and raised in Germany. We spoke English at home, but I'm sure it wasn't perfect, perhaps with a verb out of place here and there (syntax like that was perfectly fine in my parents' native tongues of Lakota and German). However, these challenges never stopped me from dreaming of becoming a children's author.

One day a newspaper article and photo arrived in the mail, sent by a cousin in my mother's hometown of Kenel, located on the Standing Rock Reservation. The World War II-era photo included my mother's uncle John Bear King and five other men who, according to the article, served in the First Cavalry Division. The reporter, Avis Little Eagle, had interviewed the last surviving man in the picture. The veteran revealed a secret he had been holding on to for fifty years: those six men and one other who was missing from the photo were Indian Code Talkers.

I witnessed Mom open the envelope and read the note and article at her kitchen table. We had no idea what code talking was at the time. I was a teacher by then, so I brought the article into my classroom to share with my students and colleagues. I knew the story was important enough to warrant some digging. I wanted to make sure our family's history was documented for my daughters. What I didn't realize that day was how long it would take me to verify and document the fact that my great-uncle John Bear King was a Code Talker in World War II.

I started with the first bit of factual information I had: the reporter's name. I phoned her and asked a few questions and received the contact information of the man she interviewed. I called Philip "Stoney" LaBlanc several times, interviewing him about his experience. He was in his late seventies or early eighties, so his memory was dim on certain details. Looking back, I probably wasn't asking the right questions. I knew very little about the war and code talking. I moved on to another approach and searched the library. I looked in the reference section and found . . . nothing. I turned to the local veteran's office, where veterans service administrator John Edmunds provided me with an address for the First Cavalry Association offices in Texas. I wrote an ad for their newsletter asking for help, and lo and behold, someone answered. John Gibbons Langan, nicknamed Jack, sent me a letter confirming that code talking was used in World War II and that he witnessed it.

Jack was a writer, a journalist, and a guide at Yellowstone National Park. We corresponded by phone and by mail for a time, and then my mom and I traveled to Jackson Hole, Wyoming, to meet him in person. He shared photocopied records, articles, and maps he had collected over the years. Jack also announced that he had two goals for me as I began this project. "You should learn the [Lakota] language," he told me first. Then he said, "You must set the record straight."

I stayed in touch with Jack after we left Wyoming. With each phone call and letter, he insisted, "Set the record straight." I admit I didn't really understand what that would entail. I had no idea that I was about to embark on a twenty-year journey.

Shortly after meeting with Jack, the Internet become a popular search tool, so I posted on forums and sent emails. I went back to the library and ordered books on the First Cavalry Division in World War II through Interlibrary Loan. I followed trails of breadcrumbs wherever I could find them. When I learned the First Cavalry Division Association was having a reunion in Buffalo, New York, my uncle Claude Black Cloud and I drove to meet Capt. Donald Walton of the 302nd Reconnaissance Troop, who was Great-Uncle John Bear King's commanding officer. On a different trip, my mom and I visited the National Archives in Washington, DC, and I made copies of everything I could get my hands on in the First Cavalry World War II files. I pored over boxes and papers and maps and photos—shelves upon shelves of documents.

I continued to use the Internet and located a page authored by Liz Pollard, a petition to have all American Indian Code Talkers recognized for their service. She referenced Dr. William Meadows, now a professor of anthropology at Missouri State University. I contacted both of them, and more new friendships were born. Dr. Meadows has helped me make sense of Jack's request. His book *The Comanche Code Talkers of World War II* laid out all code-talking groups chronologically. The Comanches and the Choctaws actually had Code Talkers who served in World War I. They, along with some unnamed Sioux Code Talkers, were the first to be used by the United States in the Great War. Dr. Meadows's book carefully details the timeline and style of all code-talking groups utilized in both World War I and World War II.

My main goal at the start of this journey was to verify my great-uncle John Bear King's service as a Code Talker. Over these last decades, I have researched and researched, turning over every stone and documenting every detail I could find. I reached out to professionals in the field time and time again. I pieced together the journey these seven men took while serving in the First Cavalry Division the best I could. Along the way, I discovered that my cousin Frank White Bull, who is a descendent of Sitting Bull, submitted ideas for a design for the Standing Rock Sioux Tribe Code Talker Congressional Medal. In the weeks before the Congressional Medal ceremonies in 2013, his grandfather, George Sleeps From Home, was identified as a World War I Code Talker. I find it fitting that the Lakota Code Talker story begins and ends with Sitting Bull.

In the area of military terms, I made every effort to understand the military lingo in the historical documents and tried to deliver proper military terminology in my own writing to the best of my ability. I likewise did all in my power to reach out to and gather information from military personnel to put this puzzle together and make sure the details were correct.

Stoney LaBlanc used the term "Lakota Code Talkers" in a 1994 interview in the *Lakota Country Times*—the first interview ever given by one of the

Frank White Bull and Andrea Page at the Congressional Silver Medal Ceremony, National Museum of the American Indian, 2013. (Courtesy Andrea Page)

Lakota Code Talkers. He identified the Lakota Code Talkers specifically as the seven men in the 302nd Reconnaissance Troop. Regardless of their dialect, they communicated with each other successfully. As such, the term "Lakota Code Talkers" in this book is meant to include all dialects of the language, just as it was in LaBlanc's interview.

Throughout the text, the terms "Sioux," "American Indian," and "Native American" are used interchangeably. The term "American Indian" was commonly written in historical documents. When I asked Native elders which term they favored, they explained that all of these terms help in communication with the non-Native people. Their preference, however, is to identify themselves by the dialect they speak, namely Lakota, Dakota, or Nakota, or as "Indigenous people."

I experienced a taste of reservation life through my mother's stories and our trips to visit our family in South Dakota. I am still learning as much as I can about the culture and have tried to depict Lakota life as accurately and respectfully as possible. I am aware that there are nuances that may have been miscommunicated, although I hope that is not the case.

I did take some creative liberties as I wrote this book. First, the coded messages in the book are documented in the National Archive's Incoming and

Outgoing Messages file, but since the Code Talkers' service was top secret and carried out so long ago, there was no way to know if those specific messages were the exact ones translated into the Lakota language and spoken by one of the seven men. I took every effort to coordinate their position with the unit and the dates of the historical messages and took into account the types of messages that Stoney LaBlanc, Jack Langan, Captain Walton, and other 302nd troop members said were sent back and forth from headquarters to the field. I chose the messages that fit all the criteria and moved the story forward. Furthermore, the translations of those messages were written by an elder living on the Standing Rock Reservation today. Therese Martin worked tirelessly to translate and write the messages in Lakota. Some time later, I queried another elder to verify the language and make changes if necessary. Vernon Ashley told his friend Don Loudner that "although he speaks, writes, and talks Dakota Hunpati Sioux, the language in this book passed his understanding of the Sioux language." Mr. Ashley is the writer of the first Dakota Sioux Dictionary.

Being true to my Native roots, I felt a need to demonstrate code talking in action and wanted the reader to understand what it meant to be a Code Talker in the field. A scene in chapter one follows John Bear King and his partner in action, code talking. The facts in this section are documented, but I have no way of knowing the exact words that may have been said in their conversation, other than that they called each other *tahansi* (tah-HON-shee), which means "cousin" in the Lakota Sioux language. An eyewitness, Manuel Vasquez, was in the field while the Code Talkers communicated by radio and knew they worked in pairs. I chose a portion of the radio files that demonstrated an exciting scene. Though there are three types of archived radio reports (daily radio messages, radio summary reports, and operational reports), the actual radio message of that particular date is missing. I studied the files from other dates to understand the types of transmissions the Code Talkers made. Then, going back to the date and event I chose, I reformatted the information in the operational report into a radio message. The facts in that message are true.

I set out with a simple goal in mind, and through this amazing journey I have gained so much more than I imagined. Moreover, I developed a deep respect for all military personnel who serve our country and the freedoms they protect for all of us. These things cannot be stuffed into a file for safekeeping; they need to be shared with others. I truly hope I honored my great-uncle John and fulfilled my promise to Jack by sharing the Lakota Code Talkers' fascinating story. It's important to remember that all code-talking groups used tribal languages to transmit messages without mistakes. Using tribal languages for telephone transmissions during World War I and World War II worked so well that it remains the only unbroken set of codes in history.

Therese Martin, 2010. (Courtesy Alana Page)

Since World War II, American Indians have had difficulties, but the traditions of a proud culture have made progress. Tribal languages and cultural values are being taught to a new generation. American Indian people are resilient.

A circle has no beginning and no end. We are all connected—our history, our present lives, and our future. *Mitakuye Oyasin.*

Acknowledgments

I'd like to thank everyone who helped me on my journey. I hope I remember all the names, but it's been twenty years, so I'm bound to leave someone off the list. I apologize ahead of time.

First and foremost, I'd like to thank my husband, Jim, and our children, Alana, Alexa, Chris, and Jay, whose love, encouragement, and support throughout the many years of research and writing made this project possible. In addition, I'd like to acknowledge my mom, Mary Monsees, and my uncle, Claude Black Cloud. You both helped me connect all my worlds and make sense of the information coming my way. I love all of you and I am blessed to have you in my life.

I truly believe God placed each of the following people in my path at just the right time. Each person had a significant role in helping me write this book.

John "Jack" Gibbons Langan, who took me under his wing, pointed the way, and started this amazing journey.

Avis Little Eagle, who led me to Philip "Stoney" and Alma LaBlanc, who granted me my first interviews.

Capt. Donald Walton, who shared his 302nd Reconnaissance Troop reports, verifying the honorable service of the Code Talkers.

Bob and Marie Stettner, Don Bentley, Jeri Hawkins, Delores Westover, Marcella LeBeau, Aloma McGaa, and Priscilla Red Elk provided pertinent information about the Code Talkers through regular correspondence, thus feeding my curiosity.

John Edmunds (veterans service administrator), Rich Boylan (military archivist, National Archives), Gen. Orr Juneau and Harry Boudreau (First Cavalry Association), Steve Draper (First Cavalry Museum), Katherine Krile (Smithsonian), Marvin "Joe" Curry (Seneca), Rose Contey-Aiello (author), Lee Deighton (author), Betty Earth, Deacon Verne Rath, Keith Red Elk,

Lenora Red Elk, and Buddy Songey (302nd RCN) supplied bits and pieces of the puzzle. Thank you for your contributions and assistance in making this book possible.

To my support system, my dear colleagues over the years: Joe Calzaretta, Terry Dingee, Darlene Hengenius, Mary Jane Moran, Donna Randazzo, Wendy Ransom, Gretchen Breon, John Berardicurti, Christy Grieco, Patricia Hogenmiller, Larry Trippodo, and Eileen Weinpress. I am grateful for all of your encouragement from the very beginning.

I relied on the kindness of strangers, who became part of my family. I asked so many questions and was gifted with interviews, photos, documents, and friendship from: Henry Vasquez and his uncle, Manuel; George and Doris Dohr and their son, Ron, and his wife, Jan; S. Quinton Red Boy; Gretchen Breon and her father, George Rath; and Michael John and his family.

Additionally, I am so grateful for the generosity of time, knowledge, and additional visuals provided for this project from Bill Breon, Charles Scott and Mary Bennett (State Historical Society of Iowa), Robert Thompson and Karen Herod, Fr. Andrew Benso (administrator, Diocese of Rapid City), Frank White Bull (Hunkpapa Lakota), Lanny Asepermy (Comanche), Alan Unsworth (University of Rochester Library), and Cyndy Gilley (Do You Graphics).

To Therese Martin and Vern Ashley, who made it possible to bring authentic Sioux language to this book because of your knowledge and wisdom, and to LaDonna Brave Bull Allard for reviewing my work for cultural content: Your feedback was welcomed and important. To all three of you, thank you for working so tirelessly to preserve the Lakota/Dakota/Nakota languages.

Several groups of people helped me build knowledge in various aspects of becoming an author. I appreciated invitations from the Ogden Senior Center, the Brockport Rotary Club, and the Brockport Historical Society to come to their meetings and tell the story of the Code Talkers, therefore nudging me into public speaking.

Thank you to my sixth-grade students, who honestly critiqued my first draft (I promised to include your names, remember?): Rachel Baldwin, Emily Bellinger, Tracey Bunce, Steven Burek, Amanda Coon, Christine Ealy, Sara Hillman, Eric Hirsch, Carolyn Keenan, Sherry Musson, Juliann Ollies, Dan Otto, Stephanie Reisman, Tom Sochia, Alyssa White, Andrew White, Christian Woodard, and Amy Zubal.

I am forever indebted to my writing friends and critique partners as I ventured further into the craft of writing: Kathy Blasi, Sibby Falk, Keely Hutton, Carol Johmann, Sherry Lochman, Jennifer Meagher, and Jamie Moran. I am blessed to have had your guidance over the years. You inspire me.

I am so grateful to Pelican's editor in chief, Nina Kooij, who took a chance on this project and me, a new author. Your patience and wisdom have greatly influenced my work. Also, many thanks to Erin Classen, whose thorough editing and kind-hearted guidance helped me on the last leg of this project. I appreciate your hard work and dedication.

I was pleased to be part of an energetic and effective group of people working together to motivate Congress to pass the Code Talker Recognition Act into law. These amazing people include: Robin Roberts, Liz Pollard, Dr. William C. Meadows, Judy Allen, Chief Gregory Pyle and his Choctaw colleagues, Chairman Wallace Coffey and his Comanche colleagues, Vernon Ashley, Janna Ashley, and Commander Don Loudner and his Sioux colleagues. And lastly, my family and I were able to attend the invitation-only Congressional Medal ceremony due to the time and efforts of Maureen Marshall, Frank White Bull, Richard Red Eagle, and Jen Martel. Wonderful memories were made with these incredible people.

Sioux
Code Talkers
of World War II

Chapter 1

Connecting to the Past:
A Story of Home (1940s)

My grandparents all had the same advice when it came to living life.
They said, "Be quiet, watch, listen, and learn."
—Joseph M. Marshall III (*Returning to the Lakota Way*, p. 196)

Children never forget their birthdays. You might think about a special birthday and remember the details clearly in your mind. Your milestone tenth birthday may have been filled with great celebration. If you've lived long enough, other dates are certain to be recalled in great detail also: September 11, 2001, November 22, 1963, or December 7, 1941.

However, these dates are not celebrations. Still, the historic events that occurred in the United States on those days will never be forgotten.

My mother remembers the details of her day-to-day life as a young girl in December 1941. At daybreak, she looked forward to her daily trip to the neighboring farm with her father to bring home two bottles of fresh milk. Her father would listen to the news on his pack battery radio before the trip. Then my mother took her place next to him on the wagon. She reminisced:

I looked forward to my morning ride on the horse and buggy to the nearby Merkel Farm. I rode on top and since it was wintertime, I would straighten a blanket over my legs. Then, I'd hear the snap of the reins to move our big Belgian work horses and we'd be off. The wind was so biting cold that even my thighs shivered underneath my blanket. All the while, I listened to [my father] talk in Lakota, our language, about the upcoming day. My parents were always thinking of the neighbors in Kenel, the nearest village to our home. Would they have enough food this winter? Who would come today to barter, or trade, for food? I'd picture the mountain of potatoes and huge piles of beets in our root cellar. We also had corn and carrots. This was all the food my brothers and I harvested in the fall. I was happy with my daily life.

She described her morning routine further:

The morning ride was pleasant. I could see the frozen plain as far as my eye could see. There were no trees or buildings blocking the view. Every once in a while, we'd see a rabbit pop up. I sat and listened to my dad speak about the neighbors, the weather and the news. He was friendly with most people around, so he stopped to talk with them, too. Riding with him to get the two bottles of milk was a way of life for us. By the time we got home, the cream separated and settled on the top. I'll never forget how we kids fought over that cream!

One morning she stepped up to ride on top of the buggy and noticed that my grandfather was unusually quiet. That day was December 8, 1941.

The United States had avoided joining the war in Europe and the Pacific for as long as possible, but President Roosevelt's radio broadcast that morning changed this. "Yesterday, December 7, 1941, a date that will live in infamy, the United States of America was suddenly and deliberately attacked by the naval and air forces of the Empire of Japan," the president began. During the broadcast, President Roosevelt declared war on Japan and Germany, and the United States formally entered World War II. People can recall this date with ease; they can describe the speech and distinctly remember hearing the crackling broadcast like it happened yesterday.

My mother described it: "We heard President Roosevelt declare war. The day before, the Japanese had destroyed the American ships docked in Pearl Harbor, Hawaii, or nearly all of them." In addition, Zeroes, Japanese fighter planes, dropped bombs on the nearby airstrips, taking out many of the aircraft.

Soon after hearing the news on the radio, soldiers knew they would be fighting Japan and the other Axis Powers (Germany and Italy). Units like the First Cavalry Division loaded up supplies and were deployed overseas. Gen. Douglas MacArthur, the commander in charge of the First Cavalry Division, went to the Pacific Theater and hatched a plan to take over each island on a path from the United States to Australia to Japan. Manus Island, Papua New Guinea, was the first stop on the way to seizing Japan.

Manus Island in the South Pacific (1944)

The men experience an amphibious landing: the naval ships anchor and the landing crafts take off for the beach. As with any amphibious assault, the navy prepares the beach for the incoming soldiers. To push the enemy back, far away from the shoreline, they bombard the beach with artillery and machine-gun fire ahead of the planned assault.

The First Cavalry Division troopers wait in the bay. Amphibious ships, namely Landing Ship Tanks (LSTs) anchored near the enormous naval ships, provide support against the enemy poised to attack in the jungle. After hours of bullets whizzing over the cavalrymen's heads and rocket launchers exploding on the beaches, the smaller Landing Craft Tanks (LCTs) zoom through the water, stopping abruptly when they hit the sandy coastline. Cavalrymen race to the beach, keeping their heads down. Surprisingly, on this first amphibious landing, they receive very little enemy fire. The naval support helps clear the way for a safe beach landing.

Then the cavalry soldiers, also known as troopers, receive orders to move inland. They climb around large craters on the beach and under broken coconut tree limbs snapped like toothpicks. The troopers make their way to the dense forest and establish a safe perimeter, secured by barbed wire fencing. The area outside of the fence is considered enemy territory. The goal is to take control of the island from the Japanese soldiers and hold on to the area at all costs.

Days later, a headquarters tent is set up within the perimeter. Inside, eighteen-year-old cavalry soldier John Bear King is responsible for interpreting coded messages by radio. He waits to hear from a fellow soldier who is scouting behind enemy lines. The message will be the most important one yet.

John Bear King is a young American soldier from South Dakota in the 302nd Reconnaissance Troop, attached to the First Cavalry Division. John's job at Headquarters is to listen to and decode messages. In fact, there are only seven men in the whole First Cavalry Division who can communicate using the code. It's up to them to send and translate the messages correctly. On another day, he might be out in the field, like his childhood friend Eddie Eagle Boy and his reconnaissance partner Philip "Stoney" LaBlanc are today. The duty requires the soldiers to enter enemy territory and gather information, so they take turns scouting on reconnaissance missions. Crossing the secure perimeter is a dangerous job.

In May of 1944, commanding officer Lt. Donald Walton interrogates a Japanese prisoner who had just been captured and orders troops to a village on Manus Island named Drabito, near the Wari River. The prisoner said many Japanese soldiers could be found there—the village is behind enemy lines.

John Bear King looks at a tent wall and sees Gen. Innis P. Swift's lingering shadow. The general hovers over John's shoulder, then turns and paces across the tent, forefinger and thumb on his chinstrap. Both they and the radio are silent.

They wait to hear from the two soldiers in the field. John knows the men packed supplies for three days; it's been more than three days, and there has

John Bear King, Standing Rock Sioux Tribe. (Courtesy Delores Westover)

been no contact. Days like today, in the scorching hot sun, make them want to take off their heavy equipment and outer uniforms, but John knows they won't remove anything. Other days while scouting in the jungle, the rainy downpour makes it impossible to keep their socks and feet from getting wet. In any kind of weather, Eddie and Stoney must remain alert. The soldiers can't be distracted by the possibility of bellying up next to a snake or lizard. They don't acknowledge the growling hunger in their stomachs after being out in the field for four straight days. Their only focus is counting the Japanese soldiers and diagnosing their physical condition, or searching dead Japanese soldiers for documents. Reporting vital information is essential for General MacArthur's plan to win the war in the Pacific Theater.

Hunching over a portable military radio, John concentrates on the metal box and its wavering dials. Then he hears gunshots pierce the airwaves. He grabs the headphones from his neck, pushing them onto his ears. He moves closer to the radio. More gunshots.

"Hey, can you hear me?" John shouts into the receiver. "Come in, come in." John adjusts the dial. "Hey, talk to me, Eddie! I need to know you're alive!"

Finally, static blares through the headphones. "I'm here—" his friend answers between heavy gasps. "It's an ambush! I'm keeping my head down!"

John clutches his shirt, trying to keep his heart from jumping out of his chest. He hears more gunshots.

Eddie is talking fast. "I'm not hurt, yet."

Everyone knows the cost of war firsthand. Just recently, another cavalry soldier in the platoon went home in a body bag.

Crackle. Crackle. Sputter. The radio breaks up. John maneuvers the dials, trying to hear the coded message. Every word is crucial because the message from the field might be critical information that could change the plan and how they fight the enemy.

"There, that's bet—" Eddie cuts off.

John hears more gunfire in his earphones. He reacts involuntarily and ducks down.

"That was close. Eddie, are you there?"

It is hard to concentrate, but John gets back to listening; he must, for he is the only one at Headquarters who understands the code.

John knows from his own experience on patrol that Eddie and Stoney are probably crawling on the jungle floor, holding their heads down while attempting to protect their cheeks from being scratched by broken seashells, thick grasses, and wide-leaf plants. They would be concealed from the enemy, yet poised to fire their rifles and use their bayonets in case of a face-to-face encounter with the Japanese soldiers. They are hiding, trying to remain invisible.

At last, a familiar voice comes in loud and clear through John's headphones. "*Tahansi?*"

Eddie Eagle Boy's steady, familiar voice comes through, speaking in code. John Bear King listens carefully to Eddie's reconnaissance report from the jungle and writes down the message:

SECRET OP
6 MAY 1944
FROM: 302ND RCN TROOP
TO: COMMANDING GENERAL FIRST CAV DIV
LARGE CONCENTRATION OF JAPANESE. OUR PATROL AMBUSHED. ONE JAP CAPTURED. EIGHT JAPS KILLED BY MORNING. JAPS HAD PLENTY OF RICE AND WERE WELL DRESSED. COLLECTED TEN RIFLES, FIFTY GRENADES, AND THREE SWORDS. ESTIMATE 15 OR 20 JAPS ESCAPED.

John realizes that Eddie and Stoney had engaged in hand-to-hand combat with Japanese soldiers, but for the moment they are safe. And they have a prisoner who can provide more information. John hands the translated message

The Sioux Code Talkers of World War II. Left to right: Eddie Eagle Boy, John Bear King, Walter C. John, Baptiste Pumpkin Seed, Philip LaBlanc, Edmund St. John. Missing: Guy Rondell. (Courtesy Alma LaBlanc)

to General Swift, who reads it while leaning over a map. Static continues to crackle through the headset. John slides the earphones down and wipes his damp neck. A small crab scrapes along the inside of the tent, searching for an exit. Hot, humid jungle weather has been unbearable the past few weeks. Beads of sweat trickle down John's face and seem to sizzle as they hit the sandy ground. Minutes later, the general gives John a message in return.

SECRET OP
6 MAY 1944
ATTENTION: 302ND RCN TROOP
FROM: COMMANDING GENERAL FIRST CAV DIV
SINCE YOUR PATROL HAS BEEN WITHOUT FOOD FOR 24 HOURS, RETURN TO BASE WITHOUT PURSUING. MEET REINFORCEMENTS THERE.

"*Tahansi?*" John replies to Eddie. General Swift's English words are repeated in a mysterious language, a code. John Bear King, Eddie Eagle Boy, and Philip "Stoney" LaBlanc have a top-secret job. They and the four other men in the 302nd Reconnaissance Troop who interpret the code are all Sioux Indians who speak Lakota or Dakota, dialects of the Sioux language. They are all Indian Code Talkers.

Here is one buffalo (tatanka). *Can you imagine millions of these roaming the land?*
(Courtesy Fr. Andrew Benso)

Chapter 2

Traditional Life:
Home on the Plains (1800s)

Crazy Horse was quite a medicine man. . . . He rode from one end to the other
singing his song. He showed the black bullet marks on his skin . . . the bullets
never went through.
—Interview with George Kills in Sight, 1967
(*To Be an Indian: An Oral History,* p. 64)

Mitakuye Oyasin. In Lakota, the term means "all are my relations." Lakota
people believe we all come from one source and therefore are all related. Elders
tell stories to teach the ways of the culture and connect the young people (the
present), to their ancestors (the past), completing a circle. The circle is a sacred
symbol in Native American culture.

The Lakota Code Talkers' story begins with traditional life hundreds of years
ago. It's hard for us to imagine looking out at the open country of the Great
Plains, watching grass as high as your hip sway in the wind for miles and miles.
An earthy smell lingers on the waves of the flowing breeze passing through
your hair. Migrating buffalo herds extend as far as the eye can see, making
paths through the fields. The thunder of thirty million hooves pounding the
dirt roars through you. It's hard for us to imagine, but the nomadic Sioux
communities of the past found it easy to follow the buffalo's mile-wide paths
of trampled prairie grass. Their entire lifestyle depended on the buffalo.

According to a resource booklet from the National Congress of the American
Indians, the United States federal government recognizes 562 American Indian
Nations, or tribes. Each Native American tribe has their own unique culture and
language. For centuries, the nomadic people of the Sioux tribes thrived, living
peacefully and productively on the land. Then, when European traders explored
the Great Plains and white settlers moved in, their traditional life changed.

Native Americans take pride in the names given to them. One name,
though, has been a source of confusion. The name "Sioux" was derived from

31

the Ojibwe word "Nadowessi," which is literally translated as "snake." French trappers encountered the word and added "oux" to the ending, which made the word plural. Eventually, the term was shortened to "Sioux." This now-familiar word has been known for centuries. However, the people of the Great Sioux Nation prefer to be known as either Lakota, Dakota, or Nakota.

Originally, there were seven bands of the Great Sioux Nation joined together in a structured relationship known as Oceti Sakowin, or the Seven Council Fires. From there, an additional three subdivisions of the tribe are based on the dialect of the language, namely the Lakota, Dakota, or Nakota.

Lakota people, the prairie dwellers, are referred to as the Teton Lakota. There are seven bands of the Lakota: Oglala, Sicangu, Hunkpapa, Minneconjous, Sihasapa, Itazipacola, and Oohenupa.

The Dakota, also called Santee Sioux, consist of four bands: Mdewakantonwon, Wahpeton, Wahpekute, and Sisseton.

The Nakota, or the Yankton Sioux, have three bands: Yankton, Upper Yanktonai, and Lower Yanktonai.

Each band of the Lakota, Dakota, and Nakota can be further divided into groups known as their *tiyospaye*. Members of a *tiyospaye*, or the family community that lives together, are related by blood, marriage, or adoption. These many divisions of the Great Sioux Nation have one thing in common: they all consider children the main focus of the family.

Sioux culture was, and is, based on the idea of kinship. At a very early age, children learned the ways of Sioux life from their *tiyospaye*. When several families joined together under a common leader, the group was called a band. Everyone in camp had a role in the society. Young people had opportunities to learn skills from elders, who were mentors. Men in the hunting society took down the buffalo, the storytelling society told the story of the hunt, and there were women and men who butchered the buffalo. The elderly women tanned the skins and invited the young girls to learn the skills of tanning and cutting the hide in the pattern for making tipis. Stories were told while leaning tipi poles together. Young girls followed their elderly mentors around, learning how to live as women. Girls and boys learned their duties separately.

Children also learned the four virtues—generosity, bravery, fortitude, and wisdom—from their *tiyospaye*. Sioux people believe attention to these four principles keep a person in balance.

There were many opportunities in the traditional life to experience the four virtues. Young men were trained as warriors. Successes like capturing enemy horses and swimming across dangerous rivers allowed boys to demonstrate their bravery, sometimes earning new names for them as a result. Young men also learned to be fearless while participating in buffalo hunting, chasing away

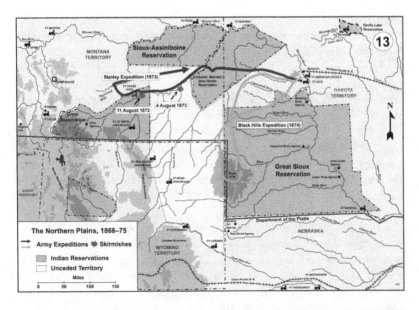

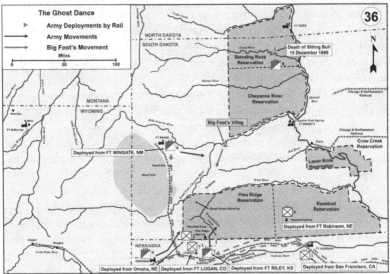

Compare these two maps of Sioux territory. How has it changed? (Courtesy University of Texas Library online)

trespassers, and protecting Sioux territory. Some boys went on their first buffalo hunt at the age of ten, while some daring young men won battle honors by the early age of fourteen.

Another important value to learn was fortitude, or the act of remaining quiet and calm during stressful situations. Young men encountered physical pain in certain ceremonies, like the sacred sun dance. In this ceremony, the skin in front of the two shoulders was slit vertically in two parallel places. A bone was then slipped in through one slit and out through the other. The bone was tied to a rawhide rope, which in turn was attached to the center pole in the lodge. The young men had to pull or hang from their skin until they broke free. A young man went through a great deal of preparation before engaging in a ceremony like this.

Young men also learned fortitude when they sought visions—dreams that gave messages about life. A young man on a vision quest might go away from home, deep into nature, for many days. The young man learned to live with hunger while being exposed to all kinds of weather. The boys hoped a vision would show a path to follow in life. Sometimes the boys didn't see anything. Seeking visions helped them learn to experience discomfort without complaining, flinching, or giving up.

Most of a child's life activities prepared him for the future so he would be able to go into battle and accomplish noble acts, like counting coup: men who demonstrated the ability to get close enough to the enemy, touch him, and then return home safely earned eagle feathers. A man with many eagle feathers was respected in the community.

In the Lakota community, one's *tiyospaye* is highly cherished. Here, a wealthy person is one with many family members. It was not hard to learn the value of generosity within one's family group. Family members shared food, clothing, shelter, and other material items. Additionally, gifts like empathy, compassion, knowledge, and wisdom were given to others in the *tiyospaye*.

The most difficult virtue to reach is wisdom. An elder's wisdom was, and still is, highly treasured in American Indian communities. Elders not only provide entertainment for the extended family through the telling of humorous stories, but they also teach lessons in virtue. They reveal their wisdom through storytelling, which is still actively used today to mold young minds, tell the history of their ancestors, and to entertain tribal members. When an elder becomes leader of the family group, he becomes known as a "chief." Furthermore, elders from different family groups come together to discuss and solve problems; this larger group of elders makes decisions for the tribes at council meetings.

Conflicts on the Plains

In the early 1800s, bands of Sioux people pitched tipis next to the rivers, and daily life on the Great Plains sustained all their basic needs. Tipis were portable homes and could easily be moved to follow the buffalo, or *tatanka*. Hunting *tatanka* provided plenty of meat. Roaming the land, following the buffalo, the bands of Sioux people moved to the South for the winter, while their summer camps were in the North. Their whole way of life was connected to the path of the thundering buffalo.

Robes and tipi covers were made from buffalo hunted only during the summer, not in the winter. Summer buffalo had skins that were thinner and more useful. Men and boys of an appropriate age participated in the buffalo hunt. Once the buffalos fell, each family member had specific responsibilities in the process of preparing them.

Women claimed a body to process. First, the brain and skins were removed. The hide, or buckskin, was brain tanned, which made the hide soft and white and waterproof. (When a hide was brain tanned, it was scraped, stretched, and dried; then the brain matter was worked into the hide to put oils back into it. Lastly, the hide was smoked, changing its color and locking the oils in place.) Once it was tanned, hide was sewn into warm covers, bedding, or robes. Flesh was either eaten fresh by the hunters or was later cut into bricks of meat and

What do you notice about the size of this buffalo? (Courtesy Fr. Andrew Benso)

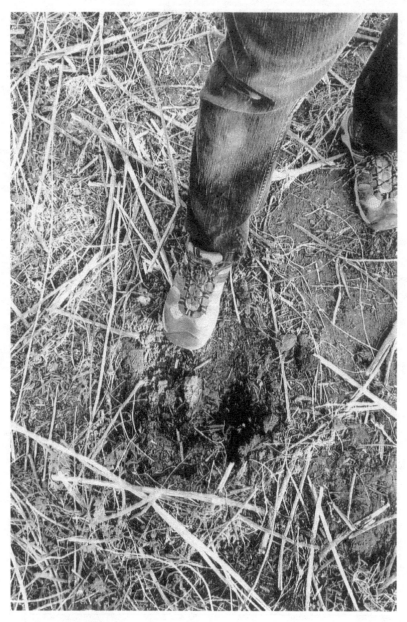

How big is one buffalo? Here is a man's size 9 foot next to one buffalo hoof print. (Courtesy Fr. Andrew Benso)

then sliced into long, thin strips by the women and girls in the camp and dried in the sun. Dried buffalo meat was stored for a long period of time and was similar to today's beef jerky. Large bones made new tools while small bones and teeth decorated dresses and other items. Sinew, or dried tendon, was used as sewing thread. And the intestines made sturdy water bags or even balloons for playtime. Bands of the Sioux people lived a productive, peaceful, and self-sufficient nomadic life.

Warriors protected their people and their way of life. Defending Mother Earth was high priority. She sustains all life. People do not own her but must care for her, protect her. She is plentiful, providing buffalo in the millions. If anyone threatened the family group or Mother Earth, the cries of the Indian war whoop swirled in the winds. Then warriors rode into battle to guard the Sioux way of life. Life on the Plains in the early 1800s was in balance, but not for long.

In 1851, the Fort Laramie Treaty was signed by the Lakota, Cheyenne, Arapaho, and other Plains tribes, clearly outlining the borders of Indian Territory. This treaty divided the Great Plains into specific territories for each tribe and promised that no whites would enter the territory known as the Great Sioux Nation without the permission of the Sioux. Battles ensued when miners and wagons traveled through Indian Territory without permission.

Then, in 1862, Pres. Abraham Lincoln signed the Homestead Act, which gave 160 acres of land to anyone over twenty-one years of age who built a home and lived on that land for five years. Many newcomers came to the undeveloped American West with hopes of establishing a home. They invaded areas within the borders of the Great Sioux Nation. The Sioux people continued to defend their homeland as the treaties were ignored time and time again. Native warriors protected their families and land while more whites moved through and into their territory.

As a result, many Sioux men were killed or captured. One group of thirty-eight Dakota Sioux was hanged in Mankato, Minnesota, for killing settlers. In 1863, at Big Mound Battle, the military attacked fifteen hundred Dakota Sioux and burned tipis, supplies, and food at the camp. Also in 1863, at Whitestone Hill, North Dakota, soldiers killed over three hundred Yanktonai Sioux and destroyed tons of buffalo meat, burned all the lodges, and killed their dogs. A second Fort Laramie Treaty was signed by leaders on both sides; but yet again, the promises were broken. By 1871, another act of Congress established that all Indian people were forbidden to leave the reservations.

Times were tough on both sides and rumors spread among the white settlers. An expedition in 1874 led by Lt. Col. George Custer of the Seventh Cavalry discovered gold in the Black Hills. This led to prospectors rushing into Indian Territory, in clear violation of the treaty promises.

In the book *Black Elk Speaks*, Oglala Sioux Holy Man Black Elk explained:

It was Pahuska who had led his soldiers into the Black Hills that summer to see what he could find. He had no right to go in there, because all that country was ours. Also the Wasichu [*sic*] had made a treaty with Red Cloud (1868) that said it would be ours as long as grass should grow and water flow. Later I learned too that Pahuska had found there much of the yellow metal that makes the Wasichus crazy; and that is what made the bad trouble, just as it did before . . . Our people knew there was yellow metal in little chunks up there; but they did not bother with it, because it was not good for anything.

We stayed all winter at Soldiers' Town, and all the while the bad trouble was coming fast; for in the fall we heard that some Wasichus had come from the Missouri River to dig in the Black Hills for the yellow metal, because Pahuska had told about it with a voice that went everywhere (p. 79).

The Bluecoats, the name Lakota people gave the cavalry soldiers, had orders to remove Indians from the Plains and bring them to a cavalry fort. Once captured, the Indian bands were forced to make stationary homesteads, stripped of their nomadic ways. And so near the end of the 1800s, when American Indians' homes and traditions were threatened by the *Wasicu*, or white men, the war whoop sounded as warriors prepared to battle against people searching for gold. As Black Elk explained, "We were in our own country all the time and we only wanted to be let alone . . . we did not want to have trouble." (*Black Elk Speaks*, p. 105) When they had to defend their way of life, they had no trouble gathering arrows and other weapons, mounting their horses, and riding against anyone entering into their territory, including Custer and his cavalry. At the Battle of Greasy Grass, known historically as the Battle of the Little Bighorn and often referred to as Custer's Last Stand, Lt. Col. Custer attacked a band of about twelve thousand Sioux. Overpowered, he and more than two hundred of his men in the Seventh Cavalry were killed in less than half an hour.

In the end, twenty-four Congressional Medals of Honor were awarded to the men of the Seventh Cavalry for valor during the Battle of the Little Bighorn. To date, this is the highest number of Medal of Honor awards given for a single battle in US military history.

Think about how the Indians must have felt. If your brother or sister invades your bedroom and steals your toys, wouldn't you want to defend your territory? Think a little bigger. If someone forced their way into your home, took you prisoner, enclosed you in a fenced-in yard, and told you that was your new home, wouldn't you be upset? Of course you would be. The Lakota people were too. So they tried to defend themselves.

By the end of the century, the United States government had forced all Indian people to live on reservations. The US government developed programs for the Indians to learn the ways of the white man's culture and become "civilized." The government sent additional men appointed as Indian agents to the Great Plains to facilitate the process. Together, the Indian agents and the cavalry soldiers searched for the last of the Lakota bands so they could round up the last of the "savages."

Times were hard for the Indian people determined to maintain their nomadic lifestyle. Sioux people lived off the land and survived by following the buffalo, their main source of food, clothing, and shelter. Documents estimate that forty to sixty million buffalo roamed the Plains in the early 1800s. At that time, there were plenty of buffalo to sustain the hungry bands. However, the *Wasicu* slaughtered most of the buffalo herds. By 1890, less than one thousand buffalo remained on the land. Lakota people passed skinned buffalo carcasses and smelled the meat rotting in the prairie sun. Their food supply was rapidly dwindling. Even so, they continued to fight for their way of life.

Conflicts between the Indians and the *Wasicu* took place throughout most of the nineteenth century. The non-Native historians referred to them as battles, titled in historical documents collectively as the Indian Wars. The Indian people told stories of massacres. The Seventh Cavalry Regiment continued to engage in warfare against the Plains Indians, particularly the Sioux. One date in particular, December 29, 1890, was a turning point for the Sioux and an unforgettable day in American history. With the conflict at Wounded Knee, battle cries of the Lakota were silenced. Indian warriors were overpowered, and Indian life changed forever.

Dewey Beard, a survivor of Wounded Knee, was involved in the terrifying events of the day:

> Soldiers were stationed in a circle . . . some soldiers planted the Hotchkiss cannon on the Cemetery Hill and brought up ammunition.
>
> . . . I will tell you my own part in what followed—what I saw and heard. I did not sleep that night—did not lie down till morning—was afraid—could not rest or be quiet or easy. There was great uneasiness among the Indians all night—were fearful that they . . . did not know what was to happen.
>
> . . . While I was in my tent, my mother came in . . . and said. "My son, some soldiers are coming and gathering all the guns, powder, axes, knives, bows and arrows."

. . . Most Indians gave up their arms, but a few were standing with their guns because the soldiers had not been to them yet. The knives were piled up in the center of the Council.

A deaf Indian named Black Coyote . . . did not want to give up his gun. He did not understand . . . what the disarming meant and then they would take his gun away from him. . . . When the deaf man held his gun up . . . some soldiers came behind him and tried to take his gun . . . The struggle was short, the muzzle pointed upward . . . and the gun discharged. In an instant volley followed . . . and people began falling . . . everybody was rolling and kicking on the ground.

While running . . . could see nothing for smoke. On the edge of the ravine . . . soldiers shooting at the Indians who were running into the ravine, the soldiers' shots sounded like firecrackers and hail in a storm.

. . . While going down into the ravine, I was shot in the lap. At the bottom of the ravine, I saw many little children lying dead . . . in their blood.

. . . While I was lying on my back, I looked down the ravine and saw a lot of women and little girls and boys coming up. I saw soldiers on both sides shoot at them till they killed every one of them . . . got myself up and followed the ravine . . . I passed right on from my dead mother . . . hundreds of bullets threw dust and dirt all around . . . the Hotchkiss or Gatling guns shooting at us along the bank. Now there went up from these dying people a medley of death songs that would make the hardest hearts weep. (*Voices of the American West, Volume I: The Indian Interviews of Eli S. Ricker 1903-1919*, full interview on p. 217-223)

The Wounded Knee Creek ran red. The smoke cleared to reveal the white snow sprayed with the blood of hundreds of Sioux men, women, and children who were shot in the back while trying to run away. After the gunfire stopped, the bodies remained, silent and frozen, scattered across the fields.

United States historical documents call Wounded Knee a battle, and twenty soldiers in the Seventh Cavalry were awarded the Medal of Honor for valor on that day.

The American Indians called it a massacre.

The massacre marked the end of the productive, nomadic way of Lakota Sioux life. Dewey Beard, born in 1862, was an old man when he told his eyewitness account to his own children. He finished his story of the Massacre at Wounded Knee by saying, "Never let your boys enlist in the Army. They killed your grandparents."

A Civil War veteran, Eli S. Ricker, realized the severe predicament of the Indian people. In the early 1900s, he interviewed Lakota people for his manuscript titled "The Final Conflict Between the Redmen and the Palefaces," which documented the events of December 29, 1890, from the Indians' point of view. Dewey Beard and his brother, Joseph Horn Cloud, shared their eyewitness accounts of Wounded Knee and its aftermath. Ricker set the scene:

The harsh winter of 1890 on the Plains made life difficult for the American Indians. The free nomads traveled together with their family groups, but with the buffalo herds gone and having few provisions, the people were freezing and starving. Still, bands of Sioux people avoided all soldier forts. They danced and prayed their traditional way of life be returned.

In November of 1890, Chief Big Foot's band eluded Seventh Cavalry soldiers by hiding in nearby mountains. A few Indian scouts came into Big Foot's camp to warn them that soldiers were coming up the river. They also brought sad news: Chief Big Foot listened as the scout told him about another Sioux chief named Sitting Bull.

Chief Sitting Bull was promised by the Indian agents and cavalry soldiers that rations of food and supplies would be available at certain trading posts if he surrendered. So he had recently walked his band into the Standing Rock Agency to concede to them. However, the rations he was then given included provisions like spoiled meat. Plagued with hunger, the Sioux people had no choice but to eat the rotten meat.

Chief Big Foot, the leader of the last free band, wanted more details before he and his band surrendered. He sent ten men to the mouth of the river at Cherry Creek for news. When the scouts returned, they told Big Foot that Chief Sitting Bull had been murdered. They had found more than three hundred men, women, and children, who had fled after the tragedy, wandering in the bitter cold. The decision was made to have Sitting Bull's people join Chief Big Foot's camp. The entire group struggled while hiding in the Black Hills.

By the end of December, temperatures were so frigid that icy wind froze branches and twigs, making them "pop" when they broke off and fell to the ground. In the month known as the Moon of Popping Trees, Chief Big Foot and other leaders were concerned about the deteriorating health of the people. Food was scarce and people were starving to death. Chief Big Foot was ill himself. Men in the camp turned to a religious ceremony called the Ghost Dance for wisdom and answers.

Chief Big Foot, Hunkpapa Teton Sioux, 1890, killed during the surrender of his land at the Battle of Wounded Knee, South Dakota, on December 29, 1890. (Courtesy National Archives, photo no. 111-SC-87772)

Chief Sitting Bull (Takinka-I-Yotanka) was a Sioux warrior born on the Missouri River in 1835. In 1876, he was the head of over 5,000 warriors; in 1881, he had only 160 followers left. (Courtesy National Archives, photo no. 111-SC-82600)

Marcella LeBeau (Wigmuke Waste Win or Pretty Rainbow Woman) is a member of the Cheyenne River Sioux Tribe and a World War II veteran. Her great-grandfather, Chief Joseph Four Bear (Mato Topa), signed the Fort Laramie Treaty in 1868, and her grandmother, Louise Bear Face, was related to Rain In The Face, a warrior in the Battle of the Little Bighorn. She is also the great-granddaughter of one of the survivors of the massacre at Wounded Knee. In 1992 and 1995, she and her son, Richard, traveled to Glasgow, Scotland, to argue for the return of a Ghost Shirt that was taken from Wounded Knee and sold to a museum. After negotiations, the Ghost Shirt was returned to the South Dakota Historical Society in Pierre.

The Ghost Dance, originated by a Paiute spiritual leader in Nevada named Wovoka, had spread to the Lakota and was popular with the Sioux people in the 1880s. Men, women, and children dressed in a Ghost Shirt or Ghost Dress, which was usually colorful and decorated with symbols of nature. Donning their ceremonial clothing and coming together in a circle, the dancers chanted and prayed for the return of the buffalo and protection from bullets.

Meanwhile, government agents heard rumors of Big Foot's warriors performing the Ghost Dance. Because the Indian agents didn't know what the Ghost Dance was, they grew fearful of an uprising. Agents sent the cavalry to relocate all Indian people to reservation lands. The Indian agents accompanying the cavalry soldiers tried to reason with the Lakota Sioux people, claiming that the government would provide food and supplies for those who turned themselves in.

Sickness was striking the Lakota people. Rounding up the last of the Lakota was an easier task when the people were weak from illness, exposure to the elements, and hunger.

Eventually, Big Foot reluctantly surrendered. According to interviews by Eli Ricker, Joseph Horn Cloud, who was a member of the Big Foot Band, interpreted for the soldiers when they questioned the frail Chief Big Foot.

"What is your name?" the officer asked.

"My name is Chief Big Foot."

"Where are you going?"

Big Foot answered, "I am going to Pine Ridge to see the people."

"Why do you go to Pine Ridge?"

Big Foot replied, "I am going because they sent for me."

"Do you want peace or to fight?" inquired the officer.

"No," said the chief, "my great fathers were all friendly to the white people and died in peace, and I want to die the same."

The officer then said, "If you are telling me the truth, I want you to give me 25 guns."

Big Foot answered, "I am willing to give you the 25 guns, but I am afraid you will do some harm to my people. Wait till we get to the Agency and we will decide as we please. I will give you all you ask and will return to my home." Big Foot's strength was failing; he spoke slowly and in faltering accents.

The officer said, "All right," and extending his arm, the two shook hands. *(Voices of the American West, Volume I: The Indian Interviews of Eli S. Ricker 1903-1919,* p. 197)

With the surrender, the Sioux people rode in wagons or on horseback toward the soldiers' camp at Wounded Knee, about five miles away. Cavalry soldiers flanked each side of the procession. A critically ill Big Foot lay in the first wagon underneath the white flag of surrender flapping in the icy wind. They arrived before sundown and saw soldiers armed with rifles surrounding the camp area. A cavalry officer named Major Whiteside reported the capture of Chief Big Foot, 120 men, and 250 women and children. The Ghost Dancers were in custody.

After the Wounded Knee Massacre, assaults on the "savages" didn't stop. During the first part of the twentieth century, Indian children were taken from their homes and moved to government-run boarding schools. Upon arrival, their Native clothes were taken and they were given uniforms. Long hair was cut short. Their names were changed. They were forbidden to speak to each other in their Native tongue and punished if they spoke their own language. The children learned English and were taught to be "civilized."

According to the Cambridge Dictionary online, "a civilized society or country has a well developed system of government, culture, and way of life and that treats the people who live there fairly." At this point, America's indigenous people were not being treated fairly. At the turn of the century, some people gained citizenship through land allotments that distributed shares of reservation land to tribal members. Some men became citizens only after they had served in the military during World War I. Then, finally, in 1924, Congress granted citizenship to all of America's indigenous people with the Indian Citizenship Act.

Joining the Armed Forces

Fast forward to 1941.

When the United States entered World War II, thousands of American Indian men volunteered, joining the army, the navy, the marines, and the air force. The American Indian people fought with purpose, and they answered the call to defend their homeland.

According to the Selective Service, 5,000 American Indians had enlisted before the Japanese bombed Pearl Harbor in December 1941. By the summer of 1942, 7,500 Indian men joined the armed forces, and at the beginning of 1945, the numbers had risen to 22,000. Army officials acknowledged that if the population of eligible males had enlisted in the same proportions as that of the American Indian men, then the draft would not have been necessary. In addition, many elderly men and women volunteered to work in factories on the home front, even though these factory jobs took them off the reservation and away from their families. American Indians further supported the war effort by purchasing over $50 million in war bonds.

American Indian soldiers, including the Lakota Code Talkers, were trained to shoot rifles, instead of using bows and arrows. The young soldiers had superior scouting abilities. In the book *Crossing the Pond: Native American Effort in WWII* by Jere' Bishop Franco, *Washington Post* reporter Jack Durant quoted a military leader who trained two thousand Indians at his post. Maj. Lee Gilstrap of Oklahoma said, "The Indian is the best damn soldier in the Army."

Young Indian men joined the battle alongside the same people who just fifty years prior had tried to annihilate their families. They chose to fight with the same people who moved them into a confined space and ordered them not to leave. The same people took young children away from their parents, forced them to live at a foreign school, learn a new language, and abandon their own culture, ultimately stripping them of their Indian identities. Why would these young American Indians volunteer to fight in World War II?

This was not the only question that arose in my mind as I began researching the Code Talkers. Uncle John Bear King and the other Sioux men in the 302nd Reconnaissance Troop of the First Cavalry Division completed specialized, top-secret training, specifically in reconnaissance maneuvers. They then received their orders: to use their tribal language to send messages in code. They were *ordered* to speak to each other in their own language. Why would the government that stifled Sioux conversations a few years earlier mandate use of Native languages to help fight the enemy?

When I looked back and discovered that the small group of seven Sioux Indian soldiers from South Dakota *chose* to fight for the United States in World War II, I was astonished. As I kept digging for information and learned that they used their native language for the good of others, I was overflowing with pride. Nonetheless, one question lingered with me. When their people had suffered so much at the hands of the Seventh Cavalry during Wounded Knee, why would these Sioux ever specifically join the cavalry during World War II?

Chapter 3

Warriors in the First Cavalry Division: Joining the Seventh (1941-1944)

The time will come when you put paint on your face. You will always stand for the elderly and the children, for they are helpless. You will not hold a grudge against any man; you must always look back and know where you come from. You will go into battles. Someday a lot of your brothers will join you to stand up for this country and a lot of them will not come back. But when you come back you will be a warrior and receive an eagle feather. You will fly like two eagles in the sky. When the time comes that one of you must go home, the other must continue what has been given, the right of life for people.
—Floyd Looks for Buffalo Hand (*Learning Journey on the Red Road*, p. 41-42)

In 1941, the year the Japanese attacked Pearl Harbor, John Gibbons Langan, better known to his friends as Teton Jack, lived in Wyoming. Half white and half Lakota, Langan had lived with his mother on a reservation in South Dakota until he was a teenager. He learned the Lakota ways of life and how to speak the Lakota language. He was considered non-Native to the outside world because of his fair skin.

In Wyoming, Langan worked as a Park Ranger in Yellowstone National Park. The summer of 1941 proved to be uneasy because the world was at war in Europe and the Pacific Islands. The United States had not yet entered the war, but a number of young Americans had already enlisted to help fight the Axis Powers. After the president declared war on Japan in December of 1941, Teton Jack volunteered to join the service.

During World War II, young American men joined the military in two ways: they enlisted, which meant they joined voluntarily, or they were drafted, which meant they were required by the government to report for military duty. Large numbers of American Indians waited shoulder to shoulder, standing in line for hours to sign up to fight for their country. Lines snaked out the door and around the sides of the draft offices. The Fort Peck Indian Reservation in

Montana recorded the highest percentage of volunteers to serve the United States, with more than half of the eligible men enlisting. Between 1941 and 1945, more than forty thousand American Indian men served in the armed forces. Military service was an opportunity to bring honor to their families and was the first chance their people had to become warriors since World War I. Volunteers were ready to demonstrate bravery and defend their territory again.

"I was bound and determined to join the Seventh Cavalry," Jack declared, recalling he had heard they were the best. "I wanted to find out how they became so strong, so I hitchhiked all the way to Texas to enlist." He documented his journey from Wyoming:

Friday, July 18, 1941: Yellowstone Park
Decided to go down to Fort Bliss and enlist. Finished my last shift for the Y.P. Co. today and had them send my paycheck to my family in South Dakota. So long Yellowstone!

Saturday, July 19: Moran
Stopped at Flagg Ranch, two miles outside the Park's entrance to say hello and good-bye to Hank Steingraeber. He offered me a wrangling job but I declined it and told him I was going to "wrangle" for the U.S. Army. We had a good laugh at that.

Sunday, July 20: Moran
Went down to Jackson today. Not many people in town, despite the fine weather.
Looked for some mosquito lotion at Jackson Drugs. They had Sta-Away, Flit, India Oil, Oil of Citronella, and Mosquitone from 15 to 50 cents. I got a bottle of Oil of Citronella, as I like the smell and it reminds me of home. It cost 15 cents.
Went to Mercill's to see what they had and found a pair of Shoshone Indian gloves, with a little beading on them for only $1.50. Thought I'd buy them for riding those Army horses.

Monday, July 21: Ethete
This morning early . . . got a ride with the mail truck and . . . caught a ride with some tourists going to Lander. They couldn't believe the distances on the Reservation.
About a half-mile from the fort, I came to the Ethete Road on the left . . . and soon got a ride with Ed Hines, the white trader at the junction. . . . Hines let me off at the junction of the Ethete and Lander roads and I walked a quarter of a mile east to where I could see the tall, forked cottonwoods.

I walked around the grounds and saw many friends . . . went by the "shade" of the dance priest Ben Friday to pay my respects and told him I was going down to Texas to enlist in the Cavalry. He said that the men and women of the Rabbit Lodge would offer prayers tonight for all the boys who were going.

Wednesday, July 23: Lander
I went over to Lincoln Street, where the National Guard Armory is located, to find out some more about the Cavalry. The armory was empty and so were the stables out at the edge of town.

Thursday, July 24: Notes on the Road
Got a ride from a trucker at the edge of town going right down to Denver! What luck!
We stopped in Rawlins for gas. Best we could find was 15 cent a gallon . . . pretty high for regular but it was on the Lincoln Highway (U.S. 30) so I guess it was to be expected.
. . . As we approached the hills above Virginia Dale, I looked out the window and saw a dark-grey timber wolf loping along side [*sic*] the truck, as though to say good-bye, and I thought, "So long, Wyoming. I'll miss you."

John Gibbons Langan, also known as Teton Jack, an Oglala Lakota from Pine Ridge Reservation, at this home in Jackson Hole, Wyoming, 1996. (Courtesy Andrea Page)

Teton Jack served as a guide in Yellowstone Park during our visit with him in 1996. Left to right: Mary Monsees, Teton Jack, Andrea Page. (Courtesy Andrea Page)

In World War II, the average age of American Indian men enlisting in the military was eighteen. American laws required volunteers to be eighteen years old or older, but American Indian custom allowed fourteen-year-olds to become warriors, so occasionally youths lied about their age. Some were as young as sixteen years old.

Once the men enlisted, they said goodbye to the reservation and went off to basic training. Like Teton Jack, John Bear King, Stoney LaBlanc, and Eddie Eagle Boy, other American Indian men volunteered to join the First Cavalry. They said goodbye to their families, rode a train to the draft office, and then took a bus to basic training at Fort Bliss, Texas.

American Indian men performed well in military training exercises. Basic training was an easy task for the agile young Indians. Some excelled in scouting maneuvers, which included climbing, running, and crawling. They learned the basics of hand-to-hand combat with bayonets. Some excelled in shooting rifles and guns. These various skills made American Indians perfectly suited to become Code Talkers. Code Talkers needed to be quick and stealthy scouts who could get into enemy territory, gather information, and get out without being seen. The main objective during reconnaissance missions was to remain invisible—hidden to the enemy—since the job took soldiers across enemy lines. But if they did come face to face with an enemy, they needed to protect themselves. Thus, specialized training was imperative.

Even though the young Indian men excelled in basic training, the government didn't want an all-Indian unit. As a result, the eager young soldiers were separated into small groups and placed in various units. Seven Sioux Indians were sent to the Fifth and Seventh Cavalry units, which were part of the First Cavalry Division. After six weeks of basic training, the First Cavalry Division received orders to report to Camp Stoneman, California.

Once at Camp Stoneman, one hundred thousand soldiers, also known as troopers, boarded the USS *Washington* and the USS *Monterey* with supplies. On July 3, 1943, they set sail on a three-week journey. "We took the troop ship all the way down the coast to South America, to Chili [*sic*], then across to Brisbane, Australia," Langan remembered. On board, the men ate together in the mess hall, cleaned, and readied their artillery. They sat on deck playing cards to pass the time. They looked ahead, viewing the vast Pacific Ocean in front of them. For the Indian men who had never left the reservation, cruising the ocean was an act of bravery. Sailing into the unknown, with Mother Earth as they knew it disappearing behind them, was an experience.

This was a time when the virtue of fortitude must have come in handy. The immense ship was over six hundred yards in length. That's as big as six football fields lined up end to end. Depending on the weather, waves may have been six to eight feet high. Even huge vessels like these hefty naval ships would feel the swell and release of the waves. It's almost the same feeling you would have if you rode a rollercoaster with twists and turns. Years of practicing helped the seven Sioux men on this first trip in 1943, as well as on any future naval transport cruises.

The First Cavalry Division was slowly making its way to its ultimate destination: the war in the Pacific Theater, where they would fight the Japanese. So far, all of the troopers' training had occurred on flat, grassy, dusty ground on the mainland of the United States. Japanese-held territories were jungle-like. The men needed training on terrain similar to the islands in the Pacific. Hence their stop in the port of Brisbane.

The troops disembarked and unloaded supplies. Men in white T-shirts lined up, and one by one boxes of food supplies, rope, ammunition, guns, uniforms, and tents passed from one trooper to the next all the way to the trains. Once the train cars were packed, soldiers traveled north to Camp Strathpine, about an hour away. The camp would be their home away from home for the next six weeks. Their top-secret training prepared them for tactical strategies in jungle warfare. "All the troops gathered there," Teton Jack remembered. "We didn't take our horses. We had to learn to fight on foot." Originally a horse cavalry, the First Cavalry Division used horses as their main transportation prior to 1941. However, just before World War II, the cavalry was dismounted. The new

Jack in uniform on his horse, circa 1996. (Courtesy Andrea Page)

Christmas card from Jack, 1998. (Courtesy Andrea Page)

orders designated the cavalry as an infantry unit. Traditionally, infantrymen fight on foot. The dismounted soldiers traded in their mounts for jeeps, trucks, and tanks. The intensive physical training primed the men's surveillance skills and readied them for face-to-face combat. But even though the men went into battle on foot and were considered an infantry unit, they were granted the privilege of officially remaining a cavalry division.

Camp Strathpine was the perfect place to learn a combination of water and land maneuvers along the coastline. Australia's tropical area includes jungle-like forests with access to sandy beach shorelines, a similar setting to the islands in the South Pacific that were under Japanese control. The men learned combat strategies in the forests as well as amphibious landing maneuvers at nearby Moreton Bay.

The whole First Cavalry Division practiced landing on shore and unloading their vessel. Grounding a Landing Craft Tank, or LCT, could be dangerous in a firefight with the enemy. Once the LCT dug into the beachhead, causing an abrupt stop, the front end dropped like a drawbridge, creating a bridge onto land. Troopers unloaded before the door hit the sand, splashing their way into water, prepared to engage in a shootout with enemy soldiers if needed. They practiced running onto the beach, throwing their bodies down in the sand, and rolling up next to a tuft of grass for cover. This scenario was part of the specialized amphibious training. These training maneuvers were top-secret.

When General MacArthur arrived in Brisbane to inspect his troops, no

A jeep hauls a half-ton trailer aboard the Landing Ship Tank (LST) from the beach in Queensland, Australia, during an amphibious operation in 1943. (Courtesy National Archives, photo no. 111-SC-242230)

Discussion of jungle training of the First Cavalry Division at Camp Strathpine in Brisbane, Australia, 1943. Left to right: Lt. Col. Charles H. Morehouse, aide to Gen. MacArthur; Col. M. Hoffman, commanding officer of the Fifth Cavalry Regiment; Maj. Gen. Innis P. Swift, commanding general of the First Cavalry Division; Gen. Douglas MacArthur, commander in chief of the Southwest Pacific Area. (Courtesy National Archives, photo no. 111-SC-192404)

introduction was needed. Everyone recognized him wearing his trademark black-brimmed hat and aviator sunglasses. Gnawing on a corncob pipe, he stepped ashore. General MacArthur was the man in charge of the entire First Cavalry Division in the Pacific Theater.

MacArthur had a combat plan: to island-hop all the way to Japan, capturing each of those islands as they went. Invading the Japanese-held territories and defeating Japan was the number-one goal. Looking at maps and analyzing data about the islands under Japanese control, the general and his advisors made predictions about the population of enemy soldiers on each island. They chose New Guinea as the first beach to invade; situated just north of Australia and covering more than three hundred thousand square miles, it is the second largest island in the world. After that, the First Cavalry Division would continue to move north to the islands of Leyte and Luzon, making their way to Japan. The First Cavalry, along with other US army and marine divisions, would zig-zag across the Pacific Ocean, conquering island after island, making their way to Japan.

During missions, commanding officers had to wait for feedback from the scouts in the field. Army engineers laid phone lines by hand and connected the wires to an energy source; soldiers then cranked battery packs to provide electricity for a portable phone. Scouts collected information over several weeks and relayed the messages by radio. From there, the generals made decisions about what maneuvers to make next. It was the fastest way to communicate at the time, but generals knew the figures did not have real-time accuracy. Still, they used the information to make the best decisions based on what they knew.

As the war in the Pacific continued, another general in the First Cavalry, Gen. Innis P. Swift, commander of the Second Brigade, met with General MacArthur to discuss how the army's communication in the field could be stronger. While in Australia, seven cavalry soldiers, all Sioux Indians, were pulled aside and given new orders. The March/April 1999 edition of *The Saber,* the First Cavalry Division Association newspaper, quoted General MacArthur's orders: "You Sioux were good in battle. Past generations of your people used to fight against us, but now you are going to fight in a different way for us." The men were selected from the Fifth and Seventh Regiments and reassigned to a newly established cavalry unit called the 302nd Reconnaissance Troop. Troopers John Bear King, Eddie Eagle Boy, Walter C. John, Philip "Stoney" LaBlanc, Baptiste Pumpkin Seed, Guy Rondell, and Edmund St. John were reassigned as radio operators and reconnaissance scouts so they could speak Lakota, a Sioux language, to each other and use it as a tool against the enemy. According to the article in *The Saber,* "They were sworn to secrecy and asked to be 'code talkers' for the 1st Cav. Div. and communicate on the radio with fellow Trp. Commanders and US Allies." The Lakota Code Talkers worked as a team and had a nickname in the First Cavalry—"MacArthur's Boys."

According to Stoney LaBlanc, everyone knew MacArthur's Boys had priority over the radio waves. Stoney explained that they didn't need special code names because they recognized each other's voices on the radio, just like hearing a familiar voice on the telephone. When one of the Lakota Code Talkers said "*tahansi,*" or "cousin," the one answering the call knew who was speaking.

The Lakota Code Talkers and the rest of the First Cavalry Division finished their specialized training in Australia and had time to rest for a bit. At the end of the six-week session, the division chose to put on a parade for their Australian

---

The Sioux Code Talkers of the 302nd
Reconnaissance Troop (MacArthur's Boys):

John Bear King	Standing Rock Sioux Tribe
Eddie Eagle Boy	Cheyenne River Sioux Tribe
Walter "Cody" John	Santee Sioux Tribe
Philip "Stoney" LaBlanc	Cheyenne River Sioux Tribe
Baptiste Pumpkin Seed	Oglala Sioux Tribe
Guy Rondell	Sisseton-Wahpeton Sioux Tribe
Edmund St. John	Crow Creek Sioux Tribe

---

hosts. Since the troopers were not going to be using horses anymore, it made sense to put their horses on display. The First Cavalry Division mounted their horses. The parade through the streets of Brisbane celebrated the support of the Australian community and allowed the men to showcase their equestrian skills one last time. From this point on, the First Cavalry Division would be riding mechanized vehicles.

The Australian people knew the Americans were in their country preparing to defend their freedom, too, and so they showed their support by lining the streets of Brisbane. The confident cavalry galloped through the streets. The event was a small reward, an honor, and a brief respite from the turmoil in nearby New Guinea, which the Japanese had already invaded. The cavalrymen carried this memory with them throughout the Pacific conflict of World War II.

———

The 302nd Reconnaissance Troop was unique. Generally, once a troop was assigned to a cavalry regiment, the troop remained a part of that regiment. However, the 302nd wasn't assigned to one particular unit but was rather a floating reconnaissance troop. Not directly attached to the First or Second Brigade, they worked where they were needed. The men of the 302nd often traveled behind enemy lines to gather information and then relay what they had learned to headquarters over the radio. The US army knew the Japanese listened to the messages and attempted to decode the transmissions. By placing the Lakota Code Talkers on the battlefield and at headquarters, the seven Sioux Indians could converse freely in their native language on the radios without worrying about the Japanese decoding and intercepting the messages. Even if the Japanese soldiers did tap into their lines, they would not understand the Americans' messages, as the Lakota language was virtually unknown to the world. It was recorded in books but had been banned from schools in the early

1900s. Therefore, scholars would not have studied it. Only people born and raised on the reservations spoke Lakota, so there was no need to create a code within a code. MacArthur's Boys were safe having conversations in Lakota.

MacArthur's Boys took turns going out on reconnaissance missions in teams of two, investigating enemy territory in the field and reporting back to headquarters, where two other Code Talkers were posted. The other three Lakota men performed regular duties at camp. The Lakota Code Talkers rotated weekly between their assignments.

The young, fair-skinned Teton Jack was a bugler in the Seventh Cavalry Regiment, a role that placed him near the camp's headquarters tent. Every day, Teton Jack heard the transmissions inside the tent. No one knew that Jack spoke fluent Lakota; although he was not a Code Talker, he understood the Lakota messages being sent back and forth. For decades, Teton Jack kept the classified secret of the Lakota Code Talkers to himself.

New Guinea (1943)

Trained for an amphibious landing and prepared to retaliate for the bombing of Pearl Harbor, the First Cavalry Division left Australia on January 19, 1943, and landed in Oro Bay, New Guinea, on January 20. Step by step, island-by-island, the troopers were making their way to Japan.

General MacArthur knew Japanese soldiers were on New Guinea, but intelligence didn't know that the Japanese Imperial Forces were miles away, on the other side of the island. As such, the ships entered the chosen landing site of Oro Bay without resistance. The amphibious landing was peaceful and calm. Oro Bay was then occupied by American forces. The First Cavalry Division readied for the next task: combat.

Meanwhile, General MacArthur continued planning for the fight in the Pacific Theater. Supplies to land units were delivered in two ways: by ships arriving in ports and by planes landing on an airstrip. General MacArthur intended to cut off Japanese supplies from the enemy soldiers already in the Pacific Islands. MacArthur's plan presumed that if US forces took over the islands with airfields and large bay areas, then the US would have control of enemy supply deliveries. Imperial soldiers would not get food, ammunition, and other supplies, and any lingering Japanese left behind would be alone and weak. A starving, unequipped enemy was easier to attack. MacArthur's idea to weaken the Japanese seemed logical. He and his advisors—including Gen. William Chase, who was the commanding officer of the First Brigade—

studied the maps and intelligence reports. They decided to move north and island-hop to the nearby Admiralty Islands instead of moving west, farther into New Guinea.

Still, a significant question remained: Exactly how many Japanese were on the island? According to the intelligence reports, General MacArthur believed Japanese numbers were low enough to plan a surprise attack, so he deployed one thousand cavalry soldiers to attack Manus Island, part of the Admiralty Islands.

Manus and the Admiralty Islands (1944)

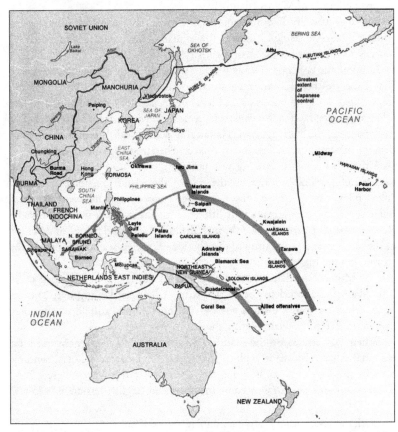

Pacific Theater, 1941-1945. (Courtesy Perry-Castañeda Library Map Collection, University of Texas at Austin, University of Texas Libraries Online)

General MacArthur decided to move and ordered the First Cavalry to occupy the Admiralty Island of Los Negros. Teton Jack explained:

> We left for the Admiralties under Brigadier General William C. Chase, with 1,000 troops, including supporting artillery and medical units, heading for an island called Los Negros. I was a bugler and orderly under Colonel Glenn S. Finley, but was a runner under Major Franklin F. Wing, Jr., as he was tactical officer in the battle.

Los Negros was located off the eastern coast of the larger Manus Island. The two are in such close proximity that Los Negros seemed like a horseshoe-shaped peninsula of Manus Island.

The First Cavalry Division approached on ships that could not get close enough to the shoreline to unload the soldiers. Groups of men finished the journey to the shore on LCTs on February 29, 1944.

At times, the boat ride to shore was just as dangerous as landing on the beach. Travel was treacherous, navigating around coral reefs and over waves. Shoreline snipers fired shots and bullets pierced holes in the sides of the landing crafts. The soldiers kept their heads down while seawater leaked in through the bullet holes. The troops stormed the beach at Hyane Harbor and took immediate control of it. Other than the snipers, they had little enemy contact. Then the troops moved inland.

Although the beach landing was rather quiet by wartime standards, the number of Japanese soldiers on the rest of the island remained uncertain. Allied pilots flew overhead, observing large enemy camp areas, or bivouacs, but exact numbers were unclear. Still, the cavalry soldiers moved forward. Reconnaissance patrols crawled through the kunai grass and palm fronds ahead of the rest, beyond the security of the division. Troopers searched for the main treasure on the island: an airfield.

The Momote Airfield flaunted a runway of flat, hard, well-drained coral soil. MacArthur hoped to secure this strip of land, make improvements to it, and then use it as an Allied airport. Seizing Momote airfield was another important step toward conquering the enemy.

When they arrived on the island, the Lakota Code Talkers went out on a reconnaissance mission to explore and search for Japanese soldiers, sending a radio message back to headquarters about what they encountered. The conversation in Lakota, followed by the translated English version, is below:

Akicita awanyang najin pi atyas' hosikahi pi icah'tki y'esni.
Lila magju. Naohoyekiye kin owanpaniya.
Makoce el psunka wognake wanice.

Onaphoyapi okihipi tayan sutaya.

Oye ota unpapi.

Toka wicasa ungnas ikiyela upi.

Ikee wicasa kin neyapi Tokawicasa kin opawinge maka iyutapi numpa tahan wawiyuta kinyekiyapi onajin.

1 MARCH 1944

TO: CG US FORCES

FROM: 302ND RCN TROOP

PATROLS REPORT NIL CONTACT. RAINING HARD. POOR COMMUNICATIONS. NO PILLBOXES [concrete bunkers in the ground] IN VICINITY. COULD BE BOMBED WITH GOOD RESULTS. LOTS OF FRESH SIGNS. JAPANESE MAY BE CLOSE. NATIVES SAY 200 JAPS IN 2 MILE RADIUS OF AIRSTRIP.

Gen. Innis Swift replied through the Code Talkers, who responded:

Egle oye ewakta oinapin el akan canker Porlaka ekta.

Wacinyan toka yawa.

Kinhan takunisni icuhtaku hantas heyabiyaya wazsijata wazsyetakeya iyaya ipawehya okaslohan ekta bleakahmni ekta Salami Wicoti.

1 MARCH 1944

TO: 302ND RCN TROOP

FROM: GENERAL SWIFT

ESTABLISH TRAIL WATCHING STATION ON ROAD TO PORLAKA. NEED ENEMY COUNT. IF NIL CONTACT MOVE NORTH ACROSS SKIDWAY TO BEACH AT SALAMI PLANTATION.

During island invasions, the Lakota Code Talkers and other reconnaissance troopers from the 302nd would sneak into Japanese territory and hide there. Sometimes the reconnaissance team spent days in the field. The 302nd reconnaissance team searched for places to cross rivers safely and sent those coordinates back to headquarters via radio. The code talkers also broadcast details about the Japanese soldiers' physical conditions. If the enemy grew weaker and weaker, General MacArthur's plan to cut off food and ammunition to the islands was working. Detailed messages helped the commanding officers make decisions about future island invasions, clearing the path from the Philippines to Japan.

Los Negros, Admiralties, 1944. Kneeling left to right: Sgt. Walter Netherland, Iowa; Cpl. Guiliford Sylvain, Maine; Sgt. Guy Rondell, South Dakota. Standing left to right: Pvt. Tom Gorman, Kansas; Lt. John R.C. McGowan, Texas; T/5 Henry Gaith, California. Lt. McGowan is from Hq. Sixth Army. Other men are of the 302nd Rcn Troop. (Courtesy National Archives, photo no. 111-SC-259248)

Slowly, the troops progressed day and night to gain more territory. The perimeter, or the area occupied by US troops, grew each day to other areas of the island.

The Japanese soldiers defended the island with guns, grenades, and deception. Many Japanese had been educated in the United States prior to the war, so they could speak English. Japanese soldiers learned the names of American commanding officers. Sometimes they pretended to be an officer and yelled fake orders out loud. At times, this deception worked. For example, a Japanese soldier once yelled, "Retreat Thorne . . . fall back to another line." When the American soldier named Thorne, a platoon commander retreated, his troop's mission was sabotaged. On another occasion, American troopers heard the Japanese Imperial soldiers singing *Deep in the Heart of Texas* in the

Radiomen of the First Cavalry Division operate an SCR-193 in their CP (command post) during the initial invasion of Los Negros in the Admiralty Islands. (Courtesy National Archives, photo no. 111-SC-192404)

quietness of the jungle. However, they detected no Southern drawl and so were not fooled by the enemy soldiers. The Japanese tried another trick by wire-tapping American radio lines and sending fake messages. An Imperial soldier claimed the Japanese troops were winning the battles, therefore attempting to discourage the cavalry from advancing farther on the island. But the voice was unrecognized and exposed as an imposter. Fighting the Japanese army was challenging both physically and mentally.

The Imperial soldiers fought with all their might to protect the Momote Airfield. Cavalry soldiers sparred man-to-man, firing guns at point-blank range and slashing with bayonets to clear the way. Allied tanks rolled into the smoky area, climbing over pillbox mounds and snapping tree trunks like twigs. Despite the efforts of the Japanese army, the Allied ground forces took control of the Momote Airfield after three days of intense fighting. Although the airstrip was overgrown with weeds and riddled with bombed-out craters filled with rainwater, it was a valuable prize. The American troops seized the treasure.

Through March and April of 1944, the Lakota Code Talkers continued to transmit reports from reconnaissance missions in the field. They radioed headquarters about anything that could be helpful for strategizing against the Japanese.

Maka oiyaye wiwiyela.
Yunkans magaju hantas ojuminyake ktesni kin okihe kasni ekle inyangkiya el
    maka.
Icu tokawicasa iykse ya peta maziylcee.
Yuhapo igluwita akan unkitawapi miyoglasin wapeqnake na kutepi yutankal
    iyuha eesnikinhan wanji wopahte.

13 MARCH 1944
TO: CG US FORCES
FROM: 302ND RCN TROOP
GROUND GETTING BOGGY. IF RAIN KEEPS UP TANK WILL NOT
BE ABLE TO OPERATE ON TERRAIN. RECEIVING JAP SNIPER FIRE.
HAVE CONCENTRATED ON OUR PERISCOPE HEADS AND SHOT
OUT ALL EXCEPT ONE SET.

Hecala oye un maza canhanpu hanska wayankapi cankuel.
Kata woyute iyeyapi timahel tipi'ikceye ikiyela miniwakpa.

22 MARCH 1944
TO: GENERAL SWIFT
FROM: 302ND RCN TROOP
FRESH TRACKS OF NAILED BOOTS SEEN ON PATHS. WARM FOOD
FOUND IN HUTS NEAR RIVER.

Part of the troopers' job was also to report on the condition of the Japanese soldiers on the island. As more time passed, they were able to report on the effectiveness of General MacArthur's plan to weaken the Japanese by depriving them of supplies:

Tokawicasa woteki akipapi, akihan wickihan iye wiceyapi.
Wita oyate kin oyakapi wakcanyan akicita kin Tokawicasa oaksu unapi mazakan
    na wahapopa kin woyute manupi wicotietan.

Akicita ospaye sakowin wakuwapi na waiyapepi toka wicasa wikcemne Tingo ikonyela Tokawicasa zaptan wicaktepi.

Akicita wicasa wanna wakutepi el kin Tokawicasa kin hetakiya napakin Itokagata Wiyoniyaupa.

Iyuha Tokawicasakin igluzepi unoyatelehanyang waposta na Toksui tunkasilayapitawapaha wopahta uhapa.

Tonakel wowasukiye ethan ikikcu pi etan wicate Tokawicasa.

SECRET OP
2 APRIL 1944
FROM: 302ND RCN TROOP
TO: COMMANDING GENERAL US FORCES
JAPANESE ENCOUNTERED ARE IN STARVED CONDITION. ISLAND NATIVES REPORTED TO RECONNAISSANCE TROOP THAT JAPANESE ARMED WITH RIFLES AND GRENADES STOLE FOOD FROM VILLAGE. 7TH CAVALRY PATROL FOLLOWED AND AMBUSHED TEN JAPANESE NEAR TINGO, 5 JAPANESE KILLED. PATROL NOW FIRING ON THE ENEMY RETREATING SOUTHEAST. ALL JAPANESE DRESSED IN AUSTRALIAN HATS AND CARRIED U.S. JUNGLE PACKS. SEVERAL DOCUMENTS WERE RECOVERED FROM DEAD JAPANESE.

Wawasukiye kin oitanean tipi ekta ha iglakaiyaya ekta iyokiheya wicati ekta waziyata wiyohpeyata.

Wawayaka Tokawicasa iyawa na waktaya najin wicisakib 0400.

SECRET OP
2 APRIL 1944
ATTENTION: SCOUT LEADER
FROM: COMMANDING GENERAL US FORCES
SEND DOCUMENTS TO HEADQUARTERS AND PROCEED TO NEXT VILLAGE TO THE NORTHWEST. REPORT ENEMY COUNT AND CONDITION BY 0400.

Igluwinyeya-po etka aiglaka akicita ospaye ekta Kaliokahmni.

Icu zeptan anpetu lelicupi na kipiya maza su yuhz po.

Oyakapi etan Tokawicsa tanke wata.

22 APRIL 1944
TO: 302ND RCN TROOP
FROM: GENERAL SWIFT
PREPARE TO MOVE PLATOON TO KALI BAY. TAKE 5 DAYS RATIONS

AND SUFFICIENT AMMUNITION. REPORTS OF JAPS IN LARGE
CANOE.

Kaliokahmi unkablezapi.
Oye waste na ota.
Ikee wicasa Heyapi wanica Tokawicasa el okaspe wanice.
Lethiya thn yupiya oyanhe wigumunke Tokawicasa le hipi hantasi.

24 APRIL 1944
TO: GENERAL SWIFT
FROM: 302ND RCN TROOP
WE RECONNOITERED KALI BAY. TRACKS GOOD AND NUMEROUS.
NATIVES SAY NO JAPS IN AREA. THIS WOULD BE AN EXCELLENT
PLACE TO TRAP JAPS IF THEY CAME HERE.

Akicita ospaye iyeya numpa tapi Tokawicasa nahanci katapi.
Tocas akihan tapi Ikcewicasa oyakapi Tokawicasakin mazakan na onapopa
    unapi na wicoti ethan woyute manunpi.

27 APRIL 1944
TO: GENERAL SWIFT
FROM: 302ND RCN TROOP
PATROL FOUND TWO DEAD JAPS STILL WARM. APPARENTLY
STARVED TO DEATH. NATIVE REPORTED JAPS ARMED WITH
RIFLES AND GRENADES STOLE FOOD FROM THE VILLAGE.

The commanding officer on Los Negros Island, General Chase, ordered
additional US troops to help control the rest of nearby Manus Island and
another airfield, Lorengau. From March 5 to May 18, 1944, the First Cavalry
Division battled for the occupation of the Admiralty Islands. At the end of
the months-long battle, 326 cavalrymen were killed in action, 1,189 were
wounded, and 4 were missing. The Japanese lost 3,280 soldiers. In addition,
the bodies of an estimated 1,100 Japanese were buried before they were
counted. The cavalry also captured 75 enemy soldiers.

Although the men of the 302nd and the Lakota Code Talkers used their
skills to remain unseen and avoid engaging the enemy while on reconnaissance,
they also knew how to ambush and grab the enemy without alarming the
others in the jungle. The Code Talkers captured 15 Japanese soldiers during
the Admiralty campaign. These captured enemy soldiers, called prisoners of
war, or POWs for short, were taken into custody and questioned for additional
information. Even if the enemy soldiers didn't talk, troopers searched their

Men of the 302nd Reconnaissance Troop. Left to right: Unknown, Albert B. Herod, Don Walton (Troop Commander, 302nd RCN), Unknown, Unknown. (Courtesy Karen Herod)

uniforms for any supplies, papers, or notebooks. Their body weight, skin tone, and general health were noted. Was General MacArthur's plan working? Were the soldiers getting food and staying strong? Or was their health deteriorating? This information gathered from POWs was used in conjunction with reconnaissance reports to determine the next steps in the fight for the islands in the Pacific.

Reports in the book *The Admiralties: Operations of the First Cavalry Division* praised the Lakota Code Talkers' work in the Admiralty Campaign, declaring that "the Sioux men spoke their tribal languages fluently and sent messages in the clear with impunity." Capt. Donald Walton, commanding officer of the 302nd Reconnaissance Troop, credited the men in the 302nd Reconnaissance Troop as being exemplary soldiers. Where a total of 1,189 Americans were wounded and 326 were killed in action during the campaign, Japanese casualties were much higher—an estimated 4,380 men lost.

Chapter 4

Island Hopping:
Leyte and Luzon (1944-1945)

*The soldier, above all men, is required to practice the
greatest act of religious training—sacrifice.*
—Gen. Douglas MacArthur

He gave up His life for us and we ought to give up our lives for our brothers.
—I John 3:16

The American troops were victorious in their fight for the Admiralty
Islands, but the Japanese still occupied other islands in the Pacific Theater. The
new day brought a new goal, new ground to conquer, and more communities
to liberate. General MacArthur next set his sight on Leyte, an island in the
Philippines.

Two years earlier, General MacArthur escaped from the Japanese invasion of
Leyte. His men, however, were captured and became prisoners of the Japanese
Imperial Army. Determined, MacArthur vowed to return to the Philippines,
not only to gain control of an island that would serve as a base of operations
right in the heart Japanese territory, but to rescue the men he was forced to
leave behind.

And so the troopers loaded landing crafts and naval ships and readied for
battle, eager and confident. The Leyte battle scene included collaboration
between army, infantry, air corps pilots, and the naval fleets, all fighting against
the Japanese Imperial force and its armada of ships in the Leyte Gulf.

On October 20, 1944, Col. Walter E. Finnegan briefed the Seventh Cavalry
Regiment, and the men joined the rest of the troopers aboard transport ships to
Leyte. Cruisers, battleships, and destroyers zigzagged up and down the shoreline,
drawing enemy fire. Boats armed with rocket launchers zeroed in on the enemy
and fired on the beachhead. Artillery was unleashed, bombing the beaches,
creating craters, and destroying hundreds of coconut palms. Rockets fired and

bombs exploded. The vibrations traveled, pounding the soldiers aboard the ships lingering in San Pedro Bay. The rapid concussions of one explosion after the other continued. "Smoke plumes are rising from the shores," one witness stated. "Battleships move inshore and renew their constant thunder" (Cannon, *Leyte: Return to the Philippines*, p. 60). The combined United States forces prepared the beach for the upcoming amphibious landings.

Flags were raised above the humongous ships anchored approximately ten miles off the shoreline of Leyte, signaling the start of the beach invasion. Troopers boarded smaller transports from large naval ships and headed toward shore, sailing through the smoke-filled air and crashing through the rough waves as bullets clattered off the sides of the metal transports. At 10:00 a.m., the troopers beached their landing crafts, dropped the front hatch, and splashed to the sandy ground of White Beach.

Cavalry riflemen were trained to be the first team on the beach. As soon as the transports landed, the troopers sprinted off the ramp and advanced to the grassy edge to take cover. Enemy fire pinned them down. Wounded men and those killed in action piled up on the beach. Someone yelled, "Let's get off this beach. Let's get moving." And that's what they did. They crawled on their hands and knees past the dead Japanese bodies. The troopers ran past broken tree limbs and crawled under barbed wire, chasing the retreating enemy. They cleared more barbed wire that lay strewn on the ground. Ships kept coming, dropping off tankers, more troops, more ammunition, and more supplies. Their mode of mechanized transportation, the army tanks, helped the troopers gain control of the beachhead.

Once the troopers moved inland, reaching the jungle areas, they scanned for enemy soldiers. Flamethrowers smoked them out of foxholes and blasted any camps the Japanese left behind. Sometimes the area was so torn up from the ships' artillery that dead bodies, thrust into the air from an explosion, hung from the tree limbs. The First Cavalry Division earned the nickname First Team because they were first in battle—the first team to jump ashore at Leyte and the first to fight on the ground. At the end of the day, four US Divisions occupied a twenty-mile stretch of White Beach on Leyte Island.

As the battle for Leyte Island continued, the men established the perimeter and stretched the area wider each day. Each team member supported the other to secure the perimeter and advance the First Cavalry Division, including the 302nd Reconnaissance team, deeper into the mountainous area. At night, soldiers stood guard along the perimeter around the camp. On Leyte, the Japanese engaged in nighttime attacks.

Reconnaissance teams were ordered into enemy territory to gather important information about the enemy's condition as well as their hideout locations. Intelligence reports like the ones below relayed this and other pertinent information, such as road conditions.

22 OCTOBER 1944
TO: AC OF S. G-2
FROM: FRANCIS M. HUFFMAN, 1ST LT. CAVALRY
SUBJECT: SUMMARY OF RADIO REPORTS FROM OUR PATROLS
1. Received from Lt. Vickery (voice) Patrol now at TINGIB, Highway 3A is in good condition to this point one way traffic. Native farmers say Jap party raided them at approximately 1750 Oct. 21, for food. Guerillas say Japs have very little food.
2. Received from Sgt. Rondell (voice) Entrenchment ditch East is a bunker. Some movement, not sure who it is. Time 1220.
3. Received from Lt. Vickery (voice) Native report that Japs moved inland on the night of 23 October. Road reconnaissance of 3A show that it is passable all the way from SAN ANTONIO to BASEY for one way traffic. Time 1250.
4. Received from Sgt. Rondell (voice) Ten men, believed to be Japs digging in. East trail is being traveled by Filipinos.

24 OCTOBER 1944
TO: AC OF S, G-2
SUBJECT: SUMMARY OF RADIO REPORTS FROM OUR PATROLS
1. Received 1010 from Lt. Beeson (voice). Huffman has found a good dump containing tarps, wire, food, blankets, and nails.
2. Jap plane that was shot down over point Dog (Monga-Bonga) was destroyed by fire. Five Japs in plane were burned to death. Signed Lt. Eidson. Time 1330.
3. Patrol went from point Charlie to point Dog and on to next town. Road in good condition for four and one half miles from Charlie. From there on is soft ground. Would have to be repaired by Engineers. Signed Lt. Eidson. Time 1338.

All the while, the job of the Lakota Code Talkers remained a top-secret aspect of the 302nd Reconnaissance Troop. Trooper Manuel Vasquez recalled, "We heard rumors about code talking back on Los Negros, but no one knew for sure. It was *that* secret. I only knew for sure because I was there that day." He was a rare eyewitness of Lakota code talking in action.

Vasquez explained more about his missions with the 302nd Reconnaissance Troop and how he came to find out about the special assignment of MacArthur's Boys: "I'm just lucky, I guess. [Guy] Rondell [one of the Lakota Code Talkers] would get ready to go out. He'd always take me along with him." Vasquez continued, "Usually a mission would take two to three days in the jungle. We didn't sleep well. Someone always had to be on guard. Then, when the mission was done, we went back to camp and rested for a couple days. On one mission,

Manuel Vasquez in uniform, 1942. (Courtesy Oralia and Charles Vasquez)

Manuel Vasquez, April 5, 1978. Vasquez worked as a mechanic at Norton Air Force Base after the war. (Courtesy Oralia and Charles Vasquez)

I happened to be out with [Edmund] St. John, [Walter] John and our platoon leader, Lt. [Eugene] Eidson. I saw the code talking in action. Lt. Eidson told a message in St. John's ear and then he'd crank the phone and talk Indian." Sometimes reconnaissance missions, like the one Vasquez described, kept the men in the jungle for up to seven days, gathering information so the perimeter could be stretched farther and farther into enemy territory.

When the beach area was secure, the generals donned rain gear, waded ashore, and stepped onto the beach stained red with blood. Stepping over puddles and other obstacles, including bodies, they reached the headquarters area to congratulate the commanding officers. General MacArthur surveyed the scene. He shook the hands of the troopers, praising them on their efforts. From October 1944 to January 1945, Allied forces advanced on Leyte to secure the rest of the island.

While the reconnaissance troops were out on patrol, the rest of the unit remained at camp protecting the perimeter. At times, they would come under fire from the thick woods. When the sun rose each morning, the rays shed light

During the war, George Rath of Churchville, New York, was a crew chief in the 433rd Fighter Squadron. He recalled hearing rumors about the Indian Code Talkers while stationed overseas. "The first time we heard of the code talkers was near Port Moresby [New Guinea]. Word got around about them, but you shut up talking about them." He told a story about his experience in the war, an event he attributed to the Code Talkers' activity. Mr. Rath and his troop received orders to relocate their camp. Tents and supplies were packed and ready to move to the new location. The original orders instructed the unit to move the next day, but then their orders changed suddenly. The move was cancelled. Shortly thereafter, he and other men in his troop witnessed Japanese soldiers wearing US uniforms entering the new camp area. American combat engineers had set up an ambush and killed the enemy. Mr. Rath remembered, "It was a dummy set up." If the unit had moved to the new camp, and the enemy dressed in US clothing snuck in to attack, they would have died. Mr. Rath credits the Code Talkers for saving his life that day. He stated there were many other "coincidences" like this one in the Pacific Theater. "The code talkers must have been just ahead of us, toward the front lines. They were elusive to me, so I imagine just as elusive to another country."

George Rath, a crew chief in the 433rd Fighter Squadron, in front of a plane, circa 1944. He wrote, "Not only do you have to be a Crew Chief, but also a book keeper too." (Courtesy Gretchen Breon)

on the effects of the previous night's fight. The troopers witnessed the extent of their fighting and counted bodies. Cleanup meant not only taking care of enemy fatalities but also ascertaining the number of US casualties. Daytime duties included burying soldiers in the sandy soil and pounding white crosses into the ground. Meanwhile, the perimeter extended farther into the jungle. Then, at nightfall, another round of guards patrolled the area to keep the camp safe.

Vigorous patrolling continued. The cavalry was considered the eyes, ears, and nose for the army commander. "By day or by night, in the jungle or on mountain trail, along the roads . . . afoot . . . in a jeep or combat car . . . the cavalry covers the ground—feeling out the enemy, establishing contact, penetrating, infiltrating, securing identifications, taking prisoners . . . And always paramount in the cavalryman's mind, be he colonel or corporal, is information—get the information and send it back in time for the boss to act" (Rose, *The Cavalry Journal*, March/April, 1943, p. 64-65). A prisoner of war provided firsthand information for the cavalrymen, but capturing Japanese soldiers proved difficult because they would often commit suicide before being caught.

Mother Nature also posed a challenge for the troops. After the frontline fighters moved forward, leaving the area in US control, the engineers arrived on site and had two main tasks: to prepare the gravel roads for travel and to reconstruct the airfield at Tacloban for use. The biggest conflict the engineers faced was the extreme weather: It was typhoon season, and a large storm was brewing in the south. Torrential rains were in the forecast.

On October 29, a typhoon blew heavy rains into the area, which made the roads impassable and slowed advancement of the troops. Strong winds tossed the ships in sea swells, making the unloading of supplies challenging. The wind howled, temporarily taking out radio communications. More than thirty-five inches of rain fell in forty days, delaying the progress of rebuilding washed-out roads and the airstrip. Carrying supplies into the mountainous regions proved to be difficult in ankle-deep mud. Even the Filipino natives who volunteered to help the soldiers had trouble moving through the muddy, swampy areas and over the steep slopes.

The reports from November 13 to November 16 described the scenery of a one-man trail covered with vines, fallen trees, and thick brush. No sign of animal life or enemy was recorded.

Although the Leyte campaign took longer than expected, the First Cavalry Division reached its goal by the end of December 1944. Finally, the Japanese retreated completely and the US dominated the island. General MacArthur transferred control of the entire Leyte operation to the Eighth Army, and the cavalry received new orders.

The troopers had just enough time to wash the red clay out of their hair and dry their socks before they headed out to the next stop. The First Cavalry moved forward, leaving behind a patch of white crosses on each island. The Americans suffered a total of 15,584 casualties, with 3,504 killed in action. The Japanese loss was estimated at 49,000 casualties.

The Philippines (1944-1945)

The eager and confident soldiers again began preparations for battle. After supplies were loaded onto the ships, personnel embarked and the ships left San Pedro Bay. The soldiers didn't know where they were going; they couldn't predict the next destination either, because the ships zigzagged all over the sea to avoid submarine attacks. Eventually they would learn of their destination: Luzon, a large Philippine island.

After sleeping in wet, sandy foxholes for so long, the battle-fatigued soldiers welcomed some leisure activities as they traveled. Soldiers slept on comfortable bunks inside the ships, without the pressure of being on guard duty. They showered, bathing for the first time in weeks after living in the jungle and having to fill their helmets with questionable water to wash their faces. During the day, the men kept busy cleaning their rifles and playing card games. They savored the fresh meals and treats, like ice cream. Even John Bear King had a bit of steak tartare, his favorite. The rejuvenated men donned clean uniforms, complete with dry socks and boots.

All too soon, the rest was over for the men. Their ships sailed past the highest point on the island of Luzon, a Japanese lookout point. Then, after several hours, they turned around and headed back towards Luzon. Why would they navigate so far past the beach targeted for invasion? It was a trick. General MacArthur wanted to confuse the Japanese on the island.

Later that night, the navy approached the beach and unloaded the 302nd Reconnaissance Troop on San Fabian beach at 4:00 a.m., January 27, 1945. When the landing crafts reached the beach, the First Cavalry Division encountered little Japanese contact; their strategy had worked. Shortly after, General MacArthur came ashore to inspect the troops. He had an important message for the First Cavalry Division.

"Go to Manila. Go around the Nips, bounce off of the Nips, but go to Manila," MacArthur insisted. Gen. Verne D. Mudge, commander of the First Cavalry at the time, came up with a daring strategy known as the Flying Column.

During World War II, the Japanese soldiers were identified in the field by various terms, such as Japanese, Nipponese, Nips, and Japs, as stated in the book *The 50th Anniversary Commemorative Album of The Flying Column 1945-1995: The Liberation of Santo Tomas Internment Camp* by Rose Contey-Aeillo.

General Mudge organized three groups of squadrons to race to Santo Tomas University, inside the city of Manila. The groups, called serials or waves, were to take three different routes and left the beach area one after another. The 302nd was part of the third wave. Each of the three serials set out to reach the city of Manila first. The troopers were confused at the urgency in General MacArthur's instruction, but they followed orders. The Flying Column was on its way.

The 302nd Reconnaissance Troop traveled with fifteen Sherman tanks. The roadside provided cover from the Japanese soldiers armed with automatic weapons. The 302nd's troopers helped clear enemy soldiers out of the way.

The flat, fertile lands of Luzon had many rivers that the troops needed to cross to get to Manila. But the 302nd encountered the same problem at each river whenever they found a bridge to cross: every single bridge was damaged or destroyed by the Japanese, and the Flying Column could not use it.

The commander of the 302nd Reconnaissance Troop, Capt. Donald Walton, rode in the last jeep of the Flying Column. The commander knew MacArthur's orders well; he sensed the importance of getting to Manila quickly, and so he knew they didn't have time to wait for hours while the engineers fixed bridge after bridge. Captain Walton looked at the map and ordered his men to go on to the next bridge. Time and again, this "next bridge" would also be shattered. Walton and his men kept looking until they found a suitable way to cross each river.

When they reached the Pasig River, the 302nd located the only accessible bridge just as Japanese soldiers were lighting dynamite to blast it into smithereens. In the nick of time, the 302nd Reconnaissance Troop jumped into action. While under gunfire, an American bomb expert named Lt. James Pat Sutton ran onto the bridge, cut the fuse of the burning dynamite, and threw the dynamite into the river. The 302nd stormed the bridge and pushed the enemy back. The troopers protected the last passable bridge until reinforcements arrived. The Flying Column crossed the bridge, and Captain Walton and his troops moved on to Manila.

Meanwhile, word traveled across the island that the Americans had arrived.

Troops of the First Cavalry Division Flying Column get the "V for Victory" sign and shouts of good luck in Luzon, 1945. (Courtesy National Archives, photo no. 111-SC-264209)

The locals, known as Filipinos, lined the streets, cheering and waving as the men walked past them in two lines on either side of the dusty road. Men and women in tattered clothing shook hands with the troopers, patted them on the shoulders, and passed out eggs, rice, papayas, bananas, coconuts, and avocados. The Flying Column pushed forward, walking alongside the tanks. The soldiers finished the last leg of the trek into Manila cheered on by a crowd.

Just a few days previously, General MacArthur had given his orders to rush to Manila. The Flying Column zoomed through one hundred miles of enemy territory in just sixty-six hours. Then, on February 3, 1945, they arrived in Manila and understood the urgency of their mission. A Sherman tank named "Battlin' Basic" crashed through the gates of Santo Tomas University. The condition of American men, women, and children held as prisoners by the Japanese army was a sight no one could imagine.

Chapter 5

Santo Tomas Internment Camp (1942-1945)

It is selfish to want to learn all things for yourself. Your children are most important. They must be the ones to understand. You must walk by example and attitude in the circle of life.
—Floyd Looks for Buffalo Hand (*Learning Journey on the Red Road*, p. 41)

Santo Tomas University, founded in 1611 by Spanish Dominican priests, was located on a sixty-acre rectangular lot in the city of Manila. Before the war, many Americans lived and worked in Manila as educators and businessmen. United States citizens enjoyed a productive life and made a good living there. American families were wealthy, lived in beautiful homes with servants, and had drivers escort them in luxury cars to dinners and dances at the Manila Hotel. Life was good—until the Japanese arrived.

On January 1, 1942, life changed for these families. The Japanese Imperial Army invaded the city of Manila and took control. The people of the Philippines tried to defend their country, but many were wounded or killed on the front lines of the fighting, not far from the wealthy neighborhoods. Some Americans were quick to help and turned their homes into makeshift hospitals that were filled with the wounded and dying. Blood and dirt caked the fancy rugs. Collectibles were thrown out of the way to make room on the tables where the injured could be treated. Children were handed supplies and a bowl of alcohol and instructed to pull shrapnel out of the wounds. Families toiled day and night at their "field hospital," doing what they could to help.

Soon after, the military army medics and a convoy of trucks came through the neighborhoods to collect the survivors. Another truck came through later on to pick up the dead. Homes were left in shambles. The flowerbeds along the front walkways that once welcomed visitors lay trampled. The families retreated inside and hid behind mattresses, protecting themselves the best they could against the continued bombing and exploding artillery from the fighting.

After the bombs subsided, the Japanese announced that Spanish, Swiss, and German residents were free to move around the city. All Americans, on the other hand, were considered "enemy aliens" and were not to travel in public at the risk of being killed. The Japanese Imperial Forces posted signs and announced on the radios that Allied civilians, namely Americans, had to surrender to authorities by January 14, bringing three days' worth of clothing with them; otherwise they would be shot on sight.

Allied civilians, including American teachers, businessmen, and nurses, were ordered to report to one of several different places. One in particular was Santo Tomas University. The Japanese Imperial soldiers stationed guards all around twelve-foot walls that enclosed the university, establishing a perimeter. Once the enemy aliens surrendered at the entrance, they passed through the gates and were given a doctrine, a new set of rules. The number-one rule was to show respect to the Japanese at all times or face severe consequences. All religious activities were forbidden.

Each person was provided a meal ticket as well as a room assignment. Prisoners looked at the tickets, which read, "STO. TOMAS INTERNMENT CAMP MEAL TICKET, MANILA, P.I." They noticed little boxes on the card, used for punching three meals a day for thirty days. A weekend stay had been extended to a whole month in an instant.

They moved to their rooms and found that the boys and men were separated from the women and girls, assigned to different buildings on the campus. Women and children were taken to the main building and the annex, while the men and boys were taken to the gymnasium and the education building. All in all, nearly four thousand men, women, and children were held captive behind the twelve-foot stone and concrete walls.

Rooms were cramped with over forty people assigned to one area. Each person was given specific responsibilities for the duration of their time at Santo Tomas. For example, men had to gather firewood, and some women were appointed the role of room mother, or monitor. A room mother had to ensure that during roll call each resident, even toddlers, would use proper protocol and bow when the Japanese entered for inspection. If anyone misbehaved, the room mother would be taken away and beaten. She would also be in charge of handing out supplies, like the allotted five squares of toilet tissue to each person, once a day. During the first month, rules were followed and routines were established. The three meals a day were simple but sufficient. The menu included modest portions of milk, meat, rice, and eggs. With four thousand mouths to feed three times a day, the prisoners waited in long lines to eat.

Then, after thirty days, the lies stopped and harsh truths were revealed. The prisoners were not going home and were not being released. Life changed drastically for the residents of Santo Tomas. Three days had become one month, and one month morphed into three and a half years.

Surviving the Santo Tomas prison camp for more than three years was not an easy thing to do. Shortly after the initial internment, the Japanese Imperial soldiers ignored the prisoners' basic needs and stopped feeding them. People ate their daily ration of watery rice out of tin cans. On occasion, a special treat, like a fish tail or a piece of carabao meat (similar to beef), was included.

The prisoners, now referred to as internees, tried to supplement the meager diet. Somehow, they sowed a very tiny garden of fruits and vegetables in the middle of the camp, but it didn't last the first season. The plants didn't grow. People were so desperate for food that they ate whatever they could find. The internees even resorted to peeling and eating the bark from the banana trees in order to stay alive. One camp "specialty" provided extra protein in the prison diet: internees prepared a meal of red ants, "boiled" in a jar of water left in the tropical sunlight. Often times, mothers and fathers sacrificed their scanty meals and gave them to their children, attempting to keep them as healthy as possible.

Living accommodations also transformed. At first, some internees were given simple bedding to sleep on, which included a pillow and mosquito netting. Each person had their own space of approximately three feet by eight feet for their "bed," belongings, and changing area. Some of the internees slept on desktops. Others flipped filing cabinets over and slept on the sides of the metal container. After six months, the Japanese soldiers provided some lumber and grass mats so the internees could build real beds. Soon after, though, bedbugs and lice emerged from the wood and infested the camp. The only way the internees could tame the infestation, which lasted a few days at a time, was to pour hot water over the bed and lay it outside to dry in the tropical sun.

As the camp grew and became more crowded, the Japanese allowed the internees to build shanties. Scrap wood and leftover tin sheets were transformed into 683 little outdoor shacks. As the internees' stay extended from months into years, they became crafty construction workers, building more sophisticated shanties of bamboo and palm leaves. Internees also named their outdoor living space. The shanty communities of Shantytown, Froggy Bottom, Jungletown, and Glamourville provided "addresses" for the nearly four thousand prisoners of the Japanese Imperial Army.

Inside the walls of Santo Tomas, the internees were cramped. Some contracted diseases, and many starved to death. Although the nurses, who were internees themselves, tried to care for sick prisoners as much as possible, they had no medicines to treat the people with. At times, new prisoners filed barefoot into camp. One particularly disheveled-looking group were the American soldiers the Japanese had captured at Bataan, a peninsula on the island.

The Japanese Imperial Army captured about seventy-six thousand US soldiers and native Filipinos and forced them to walk more than seventy miles north in six days, to the city of San Fernando. From there, survivors boarded railcars and were sent to prison camps like Bilibid and Santo Tomas. The Imperial soldiers brutally tortured and beat people along the journey. For the first four days, prisoners walked on paved roads, in bare feet, in the hot tropical sun without water and very little food. During the last two days, each person was given one rice ball to eat a day. If anyone stopped walking, fell out of line from exhaustion, or tried to escape, they were shot or bayoneted to death. Although numbers vary by sources, approximately twenty-five hundred American soldiers and ten thousand Filipinos perished on this march.

Some survivors of the Bataan Death March arrived at the Santo Tomas prison camp. The nurses tended to the sick and dying the best they could. They never gave up treating their patients, the prisoners of Santo Tomas.

New prisoners weren't the only ones making their way into camp. Rumors came from outsiders who were trying to help any way they could. When the outsiders snuck food into the camp, they also delivered some news: American troops were on their way. Excitement erupted inside the camp.

One day, six airplanes passed over the camp, dropping a pair of goggles with a note attached. It fell right in the center of the compound. The prisoners were not sure what was meant by, "Roll out the barrel. Santa is coming." They didn't know what to expect, but something was different. It was a feeling of hope. Hope that help would come. And it finally did.

The Rescue (February 1945)

For the past two years, the First Cavalry Division's amphibious training came in handy. They trained and fought on land and at sea. They had spent months in a tropical setting. However, the next stop was Manila, a cityscape. This was a different kind of jungle. And the enemy was ready to fight.

The first wave of the Flying Column arrived along the outskirts of Manila at 6:35 p.m. on February 3, 1945. Machine guns fired. The First Cavalry troopers kept moving forward, walking on both sides of the Forty-Fourth Tank Battalion. The soldiers and tanks rumbled through town.

The First Cavalry Division and its tanks arrived at Santo Tomas at 8:30 p.m. Armed and ready, they blasted the main gate wide open. An army tank barreled through the dust and debris, crumbling the walls that kept the internees captive. Hundreds of troopers crawled over the rubble, flanking the tanks as they entered the university.

The soldiers and tanks move forward. (Courtesy Karen Herod)

Troopers walk next to the tanks through town. (Courtesy Karen Herod)

The loud noises, bright flares, and glaring lights confused the prisoners at first. Once the internees recognized the tanks as American, they couldn't help but cheer loudly. Men, women, and children clutched the uniformed soldiers with their withered fingers. These people resembled walking skeletons, having wasted away for years on the slim, rationed meals. Compared to the strong soldiers, the internees were incredibly small. Someone sang the beginning of "God Bless America," and the camp erupted in a chorus of cheerful singing. The celebration continued, but danger lurked outside the university walls—the Japanese continued firing into the camp. The troop commanders yelled, "Get back and take cover!" The internees retreated inside the buildings. The tanks and troopers positioned themselves in the compound to defend Santo Tomas.

Another group of soldiers sought out the Japanese officer in charge of the camp, captured him, and marched him down to the main gate. He shuffled forward with his hands on his head. Once he entered the crowded area, he walked purposefully toward the center. The soldier wondered at this odd behavior; something was wrong. All of a sudden, his hands moved quickly. But the soldiers guarding him made sure he never had a chance to pull the pin on the grenade he had hidden. The American soldiers shot him first.

Many years later, at a hospital back in the United States, a Lakota Code Talker and platoon leader for the 302nd Reconnaissance Troop was reunited with one of the internees of Santo Tomas who was rescued that night by the First Cavalry Division. Guy Rondell, who became a pastor after the war, spoke with Mrs. Leonard Duerfeldt. Their conversation was recounted by the *Gordon (NE) Journal* in an undated article titled "Pastor Rondell Recalls Philippine Liberation."

"Are you one of our men who liberated the Philippines?" Mrs. Duerfeldt asked. "I am one of many men," Rondell replied.

"And were you there when they liberated Santo Tomas?"

"Yes, I was. My cavalry division was one of the first ones in."

"Well, I was there too. I was one of the people in the camp."

The article provided more details about the rescue:

"So we had to take off . . . You find the road, fin[d] the mines, hold the bridges until the group catches up and then you go again. I remember the moonlight, it was hazy from the fires in Manila." He continued, "As the sun began to rise we were on the edge of the city, but the road was heavily mined. Usually the Filipinos helped us by pointing out the openings through the mine fields so that we could get through. There was heavy fighting but by dusk of that day, we were ready to move into Santo Tomas."

Mrs. Duerfeldt continue[d] the story. "We knew something was up," she said. "We were confined to our quarters early in the evening which was very unusual. And then somebody said that they could smell gasoline fumes, so we knew that the Americans were in the outlying regions." . . . She turned to Mr. Rondell. "Were you in a tank?" she asked. "I remember that tank. Didn't it go through the wall because the gate was too small?"

The minister thought for a moment and then laughed, "Yes I remember. Most of us were in armoured scout carriers, but we had to use a tank to break through that gate. It was late afternoon, almost dark when we came in. At first, no one came out," he continued. "I don't think they knew who we were. But we yelled to them and when they realized who we were . . . It was pretty emotional . . . there was a lot of crying."

. . . Then Mrs. Duerfeldt graciously extended her hand to the Rev. Guy Rondell and said, formally, "I didn't have a chance to say it before, years ago, but I will now. Thank you. Thank you for coming to rescue me."

The Lakota Code Talkers and others in the 302nd Reconnaissance Troop must have felt like warriors that day when they crashed through the walls of Santo Tomas with the rest of the Flying Column, fighting for respect for human life and for freedom to live that life.

———

After the Americans arrived in Santo Tomas, the soldiers defended the camp for another three days amid intense fighting for control of Manila. The fight for the city was a new kind of battle. Gunshots kept firing. Smoke from burning buildings hung in the air. Broken buildings, fragments of walls, and piles of rubble provided a screen from enemy fire. Snipers hid in the tallest points of the ruined city and fired on the soldiers, but the troopers kept inching forward. Soldiers of the First Cavalry Division turned over every stone and searched every building looking for the enemy. Many dead Imperial Japanese soldiers lay crumpled on the ground.

When US soldiers surrounded a Japanese soldier on the ground, they followed a specific protocol. Troopers moved toward the body and circled it, armed and ready. Someone checked to make sure the enemy was dead. Then they searched the soldier's uniform pockets for papers. One cavalry soldier found a journal on one body. When translated, the journal stated that the emperor, who was the leader of all of Japan, had given orders for the systematic killing of all prisoners. In addition, the emperor ordered the destruction of the internment camp as well as the city of Manila. General MacArthur had sent the Flying Column just in time, thus saving the lives of 3,700 internees.

The Japanese Imperial Army followed orders and were in the process of destroying as much as of the city as possible. Buildings were burned to the ground. The Japanese hid among the piles of rubble that were once a thriving city and fought the American troopers. The cavalry soldiers fought day and night to protect the internees. It took three days for the cavalry to secure the city of Manila and to force the rest of the Japanese army to scatter. The prisoners of Santo Tomas finally had their freedom after thirty-seven months of unbearable conditions.

Once the Japanese Imperial Army retreated, the city was safe. The Japanese flag was taken down and a larger American flag was unrolled and tacked over the entrance of the main building of Santo Tomas. The fabric unfurled so that everyone could see the stars and stripes hanging over the balcony. The smiling internees waved their hands, clapping and cheering. Santo Tomas was now American territory.

The days of peace that followed were spent caring for the prisoners. Buildings turned into makeshift hospitals. Some soldiers sacrificed their C-rations at first, but then found out it was not the right thing to do. When malnourished prisoners ate normal food too quickly, their starved bodies were shocked. Their tiny stomachs could only handle so much. People vomited right away. Some internees became so sick from gulping down the rich food that they died. The children in the camp fared the best during the years of imprisonment; their parents had shared their own rations, feeding their children first.

Nearby, the navy ships docked. The troopers snaked around the rubble and one by one unloaded medical supplies, food, and other provisions into Manila. Troopers cooked food in enormous pots. To get even one scoop of food, men stood in long lines bare-chested, revealing bones covered by thin muscles under tanned, wrinkly skin. They didn't mind the wait because they knew they were going to eat. They held onto their full plate of food with two hands and found a place to sit. They spooned their meals into their mouths, shaking their heads. Now free, the former prisoners of war could count on eating regular meals.

After the war, the Philippine government awarded medals to all soldiers who helped rescue the internees of Santo Tomas. During the camp internment and the battle for Manila, 475 prisoners died. Luckily, 3,768 other Santo Tomas prisoners were freed.

The First Cavalry Division was victorious in their race to Manila and one step closer to conquering Japan, the end line in a long journey. Once life stabilized in the camp at Santo Tomas, the Lakota Code Talkers and the rest of the First Cavalry Division were ready to knock down the front door of the Japanese. A surprise attack on Japanese soil was planned. The men were primed to go.

Japan (1945)

Before MacArthur's surprise attack rolled out, atomic bombs hit the Japanese cities of Hiroshima and Nagasaki. The nuclear power of these bombs leveled the two cities in an instant. Thousands of people at the bombsites in each of the cities vanished into thin air. People who were miles away from the center of the attack ran away as fast as they could. The atomic bombs unleashed a power no person on Earth had ever witnessed before.

Japan's leader, Emperor Hirohito, surrendered in August 1945. Then, on September 2, 1945, World War II officially ended when Japanese representatives signed papers in front of General MacArthur. The peace ceremony occurred aboard the battleship USS *Missouri* in Tokyo Bay, surrounded by an armada of Allied ships. Following tradition, an American flag was raised to signify victory. The flag used on this occasion was the same one that had flown over the Capitol Building on December 7, 1941, the day of the Pearl Harbor attack.

On September 5, 1945, Gen. William Chase led the First Cavalry Division into Tokyo, the 302nd Reconnaissance Troop included. The First Cavalry raised the capitol flag again, this time on Japanese soil. American troops achieved their goal: they occupied and controlled Japan.

Troopers in the 302nd Reconnaissance Troop. Left to right: Albert B. Herod, unknown, Bud Outz, unknown, Martin Nassour. The last name of one of the unknown men is Plesenger. (Courtesy Karen Herod)

George Dohr and fellow troopers with their catch of the day. (Courtesy Ron Dohr)

Marching band and parade in Tokyo. (Courtesy Ron Dohr)

The First Cavalry added "First in Tokyo" to its long list of "firsts" as the troopers set up headquarters. Although not in battle at the time, the men were tired of the C-rations that had nourished them on their journey to Japan. Once the division arrived in Tokyo, George Dohr, a trooper in the 302nd Reconnaissance Troop, found a pond stocked with the biggest frogs he had ever seen. Dohr and his buddies went hunting, or gigging, for frogs one day and enjoyed a feast that evening.

After months of hard work in the humidity, Allied personnel earned the privilege of resting and taking in the tranquil Japanese scenery. First, though, the cavalry once again put on a display. Large formations of rumbling cars, roaring tanks, and foot soldiers marched down the street in parades meant to increase the morale of the troops and serve as an honor for any visiting dignitaries, namely Gen. Dwight D. Eisenhower and former president Herbert Hoover.

Following World War II, a Native American veteran and a Lakota Code Talker in the Third Battalion named Clarence Wolf Guts expressed his feelings clearly: "We love America so much. We will do all we can to protect it from aggressors." Looking back at the First Cavalry Division's journey island hopping from Australia to Japan, they did just that. Native American soldiers put the past behind them and chose to fight side by side with their white, Asian, Latino, and African-American brothers in World War II in order to protect their country. They sacrificed together to conquer adversity and gain victory.

The honorable warriors had come full circle, engaging in battle from feathers to sabers, protecting our freedoms as well as our homeland, Mother Earth. The Lakota Code Talkers heeded the call of duty and acted with great honor.

Chapter 6

Eagle Feathers for the Code Talkers

*In my great vision, when I stood at the center of the world, the two men from the
east had brought me the day-break-star herb and they had told me to drop it on
the earth; and where it touched the ground it took root and bloomed four-rayed.
It was the herb of understanding. Also, where the red man of my vision changed
into a bison that rolled, the same herb grew and bloomed when the bison had
vanished and after that the people in my vision found the good red road again.*
—Black Elk (*Black Elk Speaks*, p. 215)

American soldiers had fought the enemy and won. Sometimes the soldiers
didn't know where they were headed for battle and didn't know what they
would encounter, but when the war ended, they knew they were headed home.

The Code Talkers received an honorable discharge after their service in
the occupation of Japan. After being paid $300 and $25 for travel expenses,
they returned to the familiar routine of life on a reservation, living in crowded
homes on dusty land that some landowners used for farming and ranching.
The nearest cities were at least an hour drive by car. Along the dirt road,
one might hear a snake rattling in the tall grass or grasshoppers buzzing. But
mostly, it was quiet. No machine guns rat-a-tat-tatting. No bombs exploding
nearby. No oceans. Just peace and quiet.

However, after serving so valiantly in the war, Lakota Code Talkers and
other Native American soldiers met new challenges on the Indian reservations
when they returned home. The army provided a steady paycheck while they
were in the service, but now that they were discharged, how would they earn
money to support their families? People living on the reservations from the
early 1900s to the 1940s were raised on the government's plan to "civilize" the
Indians. The former nomadic Indian people were dependent on the provisions
of government flour, lard, salt pork, sugar, cheese, and powdered milk. Homes
were built and filled with wood-burning stoves and a few pieces of furniture.

After World War II, the veterans had skills and wanted to work. But when they went to nearby cities to search for jobs, they were shunned by non-Native community members. Marcella LeBeau, an army nurse and a relative of Code Talker Eddie Eagle Boy, recalled reading signs hanging in windows that said No Dogs or Indians Allowed. These young men and women had just served this country with the greatest of sacrifices. They survived battles, endured challenges of war, and earned medals so that these community members could enjoy the freedom to pursue their dreams of owning a business.

As a result of such prejudice, and a lack of local jobs, many American Indian veterans were unemployed following the war. These resilient Indian people had endured so much within the last decades. Just fifty years prior, Indian people had been herded onto a plot of land and stripped of their traditional way of life. Poachers had killed 90 percent of all the American bison by 1890, leaving the Indian people with no food source, blankets, or tools. After the war, veterans were not allowed in cities and towns. They were again dependent on the government for food; and since no jobs were available, the veterans took any job they could find farming, ranching, and riding in rodeos. They did not give up even though they faced many challenges.

The author and Marcella LeBeau at her home in South Dakota. (Courtesy Andrea Page)

On the other hand, the reception the veterans received from their own people was quite different. Each tribe welcomed home their loved ones and honored them. Tribes organized gatherings called powwows. Enormous drums framed the circle, or arena. At least four or more drummers sat around the instruments singing warrior songs. Colorful dancers dressed in regalia stepped into the circle and twirled to each song's rhythm. Fancy dancers and shawl dancers hopped and swayed to the beat of the drums. The tribal community paid tribute to the soldiers who returned home safely.

Each soldier's family participated in a traditional Sioux ceremony called the Giveaway. In Native American culture, material wealth is shared and given away. To the Lakota, a prosperous man is not one with many possessions but one with many family members. A very large family meant the *tiyospaye* was wealthy. The Giveaway was, and still is, a celebration for people to show their generosity. The Indian families came together to give away their most prized material goods. S. Quinton Red Boy, a Dakota elder and Code Talker from Montana, summarized it best: "I don't love money. I love people."

During the ceremony, family members gave away a variety of items like homemade star quilts or even a horse to other tribal members. Then the family slid into the dancing circle and shook hands with every community member. These gestures thank the members of the *tiyospaye* for their support and generosity. This ceremony still takes place during powwows today.

When a warrior in the 1800s returned to his camp victorious, he earned an eagle feather. His war story was told over and over to the members of the tribe. In 1945, the tribes honored the veterans at powwows and heard their stories— with the exception of the Code Talkers' tales. Very few people knew about code talking in 1945. It was classified information, which meant it was confidential and a matter of national security. The soldiers were mindful of their duty and remained silent about their wartime missions. Many went to their graves without telling even one family member about their special assignment during World War II, keeping the secret for more than half a century. Can you imagine keeping a secret until the time when your children have children?

Some veterans began to tell their stories when information on code talking became declassified. Facts about other code-talking groups surfaced, including news articles about the Comanche, Chippewa, Meskwaki, and Choctaw Code Talkers written by commanding officers after the war. Little by little, details emerged; the humble men began to talk about their service. In 2002, a book titled *The Comanche Code Talkers of World War II* was published by William C. Meadows, who, at the time, had identified seventeen different tribal groups that had Code Talkers who served in the armed forces, both in World War I and World War II.

Other American Indian Code Talkers—World War I

During World War I, the United States sent classified messages in code and relayed them over the radio. As the war went on, the enemy intercepted vital messages from time to time. The German agents—the enemy—were considered to be masters at tapping lines and decoding messages. American officers realized they needed a better code to confuse the Germans.

The idea of Indian code talking was first used in October of 1918. One day while walking through camp, an American officer overheard two Choctaws talking in their native language. The officer thought the Indians, Solomon Louis and Mitchell Bobb, should speak their own language to transmit messages over the telephone. To test the idea, he made a plan.

The commanding officer found eight Choctaw Indians in the battalion. Two men, Ben Carterby and Pete Maytubby, were stationed at headquarters. Louis and Bobb were sent out in the field and were given a written statement to translate. They translated the message into Choctaw and sent it to headquarters. The message at headquarters was translated accurately within minutes. The Germans expected their code breakers to decode the message, but they were stumped. Code talking worked!

Soon, the Choctaw Indians formed the first code-talking group, known as the Choctaw Telephone Squad. The Choctaw Telephone Squad included Mitchell Bobb, James Edwards, Calvin Wilson, James Davenport, George Davenport, Albert Billy, Victor Brown, Ben Carterby, Tobias Frazer, Ben Hampton, Noel Johnson, Solomon Louis, Pete Maytubby, Jeff Nelson, Joseph Oklahombi, Robert Taylor, and Walter Veach. Solomon Louis was chosen as the squad's leader; their commanding officer was Capt. E. H. Horner. Most members were assigned to the 142nd Regiment of the Thirty-Sixth Infantry Division. Two were in the 141st Infantry Regiment.

Once code talking was used in the field, the Choctaws made several recommendations for improvements. Although English terms translated well, many military terms did not have a direct translation in the Choctaw language. So the men agreed on alternative words. The Choctaw word for "stone" would represent "grenade," and the word for "tribe" was a code word for "regiment," and so on and so forth.

The Choctaw Telephone Squad experiment proved to be a valuable tool in United States history. The National Security Agency used the group as the model for future code-talking organizations.

In addition to the Choctaws, two Sioux Indians were given assignments as telephone operators in the Meuse-Argonne Offensive. These men coded messages in their native tongue for three days and nights near the end of World

War I, using a phone line they knew the Germans had wiretapped. They had such faith in code talking, though, that they were not concerned about the Germans interpreting their messages, even if they were intercepted. One man was placed forward with the artillery observer (sending the message) and the other remained back with the brigade (receiving the message). According to the Summer 1919 issue of *American Indian Magazine*, "They [Sioux Indians] and the artillery commander and their own colonel enjoyed the situation immensely."

Other American Indian Code Talkers—World War II

During World War II, the First Cavalry Division was not the only military group that utilized Sioux Code Talkers. In the Third Field Artillery Battalion, a number of Sioux soldiers were assigned to reel-cart teams. Soldiers on these teams laid down telephone lines rolled up on reels across the fields. Simon Broken Leg, Jeffrey Dull Knife, Garfield T. Brown, Anthony Omaha Boy, John C. Smith, and others were Code Talkers assigned to the Thirty-Second Field Artillery Regiment. Charles White Pipe was in the Fortieth Division, 164th Field Artillery Battalion. Clarence Wolfguts, who served in the Eighty-First Infantry Division with his cousin Iver Crow Eagle, Sr., worked together as a Code Talker with Roy Bad Hand and Benny Red Bear, Sr.

Two groups of Dakota Code Talkers served in the Montana National Guard and then in the 163rd Infantry Regiment, Company B. Though these groups worked separately, both were part of the 163rd Infantry, which was one of the first groups to secure the island of Hawaii following the Pearl Harbor attack. These two code-talking groups were also part of the only all-Indian unit to serve in the US armed forces. One of the Dakota code-talking groups consisted of a two-partner team of S. Quinton Red Boy and Herman Red Elk. According to Quinton, they radioed coordinates of enemy machine gun nests on the island to their commanding officer, and soon after their reports, artillery fire eliminated the nests. After the attack on Pearl Harbor, Quinton and Herman were instructed to remain as anonymous as possible. The Japanese, who would disguise themselves as Hawaiian civilians, attempted to get information from soldiers. Therefore, unit patches were not displayed on uniforms in public.

In addition, if Hawaiian residents asked either of the soldiers for a name, Quinton and Herman answered "Joe." However, on the radio, they called each other by code names they created. Quinton's code name was "Shigematsu," after a military leader in the Japanese forces; Herman's was "Hirohito," named after the emperor of Japan. Imagine how confused Japanese code breakers were to hear those two names repeated on US radios! After Hawaii, the men shipped out with the Forty-First Infantry Division, nicknamed the Sunset Division.

The Forty-First Infantry Division invaded islands with unique qualities. Leyte, for example, didn't have an airstrip, so receiving additional supplies was a challenge, making their food rations slim. When rations ran out, American soldiers had to figure out how to curb their hunger. Quinton explained that he once spotted an area in the jungle with ponds filled with fish and frogs. But he

Members of the 163rd Infantry Regiment, Forty-First Division, display captured Japanese sabers on Wakde Island, Dutch New Guinea, 1944. (Courtesy National Archives, photo no. 111-SC-272047)

Pulitzer Prize winner and war correspondent Ernie Pyle reported from the trenches in Europe, Africa, and the Pacific. He wrote from the soldiers' viewpoint instead of reporting on the generals and their plans. A Japanese sniper shot and killed Pyle on April 18, 1945. A movie about his life, *The Story of G.I. Joe*, premiered in 1945, starring Burgess Meredith. The G.I. Joe doll debuted in 1964, named after the movie, and was the first action figure in the world.

had one problem: he didn't have a fishing pole, and his group didn't have time to sit patiently and wait for the fish to bite. So how did he catch the fish? Quinton said, "I decided to throw a grenade in the pond and grab all the fish I could and run. The explosion told the enemy right where we were, so we had to take cover quickly." Quinton was resourceful and bold.

The second Dakota code-talking group, also part of the 163rd, included Herman Red Elk's brother, Gerald, along with James Turningbear, Joe Red Door, Roscoe White Eagle, and Raymond Ackerman. Lenora Red Elk discovered that Gerald, her husband, was a Code Talker when she read the story in a local newspaper. Lenora identified the commanding officer as Captain Duncan Dupree. According to *American Indian Magazine* in 1945, both Raymond Ackerman and Duncan Dupree were killed in New Guinea and posthumously received Purple Hearts and Silver Stars for their valor.

During World War II, code-talking Indian groups that used conversational code (sending coded messages by simply speaking to each other) like the Lakota Code Talkers did included: Canadian Cree, Choctaw, Menominee, Muscogee, Seminole, Pawnee, and the Apache. Meanwhile, other groups were trained in use of an exclusive code, like the Comanche, Meskwaki, Chippewa-Oneida, Hopi, and Navajo Code Talkers. The latter groups used a body of specially created code terms within their native language instead of just speaking in that language itself.

Several different tribes were initially considered for formal code-talking training. Around Christmas of 1940, recruiters began looking for volunteers from tribes in Oklahoma. Local advertisements listed a requirement: "Must be fluent in the Comanche language." This unusual request from the army did not explain why the men needed to speak Comanche. But it did not hinder young Comanche men from joining the service.

Seventeen Comanches were sent to Fort Benning, Georgia, for basic training with the Fourth Infantry Division. After basic training, the group went to Louisiana for more training. In the Louisiana swamps, the men practiced speaking to each other on portable telephones across huge fields. English communications were translated into Comanche, communicated in Comanche, and then translated back into English. The transmissions were quick and accurate. These special sessions were known as the Louisiana War Games.

Establishing accurate communications in the Comanche language had one obstacle. Similar to the situation with the Choctaw language in World War I, Comanche did not have words for all the necessary military terms. Therefore, with the help of their commanding officer, 2nd Lt. Hugh Foster, the Comanche Code Talkers negotiated certain words for military terms.

For example, there was no term for "tank," so someone decided to use the Comanche word for "turtle." Another recruit came up with the Comanche phrase for "sewing machine gun" as a code for "machine gun," because an automatic weapon sounded like his mother's sewing machine. The Comanche phrase for "Crazy White Man" was used for Adolf Hitler.

The Comanche Code Talkers also improvised. If the name of a city needed to be translated, the Code Talker would start with, "Now listen to this," and would then proceed with a list of Comanche words. The first letter of each Comanche term was taken; together, the letters spelled the name of the city or village in English.

In 1941, eight Meskwaki men were selected from the Sac and Fox Reservation near Tama, Iowa, as Code Talkers. They joined the 168th Infantry of the Thirty-Fourth Infantry Division and received special radio and machine-gun training in Iowa and later at Camp Claiborne in Louisiana. They shipped out to Algiers, the capital of Algeria, in 1942. The soldiers carried backpacks and walkie-talkie radios that had a three-mile range, enough to cover the distance between the front lines and regimental headquarters. The Meskwaki Code Talkers used the Indian word *okemawan*, which means "chief," to describe

The Comanche Code Talkers, Ft. Benning, Georgia, 1942. Kneeling left to right: Roderick Red Elk, Simmons Parker, Larry Saupitty, Melvin Permansu, Willis Yackeschi, Charles Chibitty, and Wellington Mihecoby. Standing left to right: Morris Tabbyyetchy, Perry Noyobad, Ralph Wahnee, Haddon Codynah, Robert Holder, Edward Nahquaddy Jr., Clifford Ototivo, Sr., and Forrest Kassanavoid. Not pictured: Elgin Red Elk, Sr., and Anthony Tabbytite. (Courtesy Lanny Asepermy)

anyone in a leadership position, from commanding officer to corporal. At least two of the Meskwaki Code Talkers, Dewey Youngbear and Frank Sanache, were taken as prisoners of war and held by the German army.

Also recruited for code talking were the Hopi. In 1943, eight Hopi men trained in a southern Arizona desert, near Dateland. The Hopi Code Talkers—including Frank Chapella, Floyd Dan, Sr., Perry Honani, Sr., Warren Koiyaquaptewa, Charlie Lomakana, Persaval Navenma, Franklin Shupla, and Travis Yaiva—went to extraordinary lengths to identify Hopi words that could be used as code for military terms. Vocabulary like *bahki* meant "boat," translated from "house on water"; *pahwewaka* meant "seaplane," translated from "duck"; and *nuhu* meant bombs, translated from "eggs." The Hopi Code Talkers first used their language in combat in the Marshall Islands as members of the 223rd Infantry Regiment, part of the Eighty-First, or "Wildcat" Division.

The most well-known Code Talkers who served in World War II were the Navajo. A man named Philip Johnson, a missionary, read about Indian languages being used for code talking in World War I. He discussed the idea with the marines, and eventually young Navajo men were selected for service.

Three factors made the Navajo Code Talkers the most recognized of all. First, more than four hundred recruits trained as Navajo Code Talkers and learned the "code within a code." Even if someone spoke Navajo, they would have difficulty translating messages because they were not trained as a Code Talker. The Navajo messages were based on the alphabet, but specific Navajo words stood for certain letters. A total of 450 Navajo terms were part of the code. Everything had to be memorized.

Second, the famous World War II photo of six marines raising a flag on Iwo Jima has a direct tie to the use of Navajo Code Talking. The marines were under heavy fire on the island and the Navajo Code Talkers went into action. With confidence, the Code Talkers spelled out the name of the attack location. The Americans stormed the island and focused on mouse-turkey-sheep-uncle-ram-ice-bear-ant-cat-horse-itch, or Mt. Suribachi. The men reached the peak and raised the US flag. Morale was thereby raised also, and after days of intense fighting, the Japanese began to retreat. This was a turning point in World War II. (Interestingly, one of the men in this photo, Ira Hayes, was a Pima.)

And third, many of the four hundred Navajo Code Talkers survived to tell their stories, meaning that theirs were circulated more than the stories of other code-talking groups. Numerous books, articles, and movies telling the story of the Navajo Code Talkers are available. When people speak about "the code talkers," they are probably referring to the Navajo Code Talkers. However, more and more tribes are discovering that they, too, had members who were involved with secret radio communications in World War I and World War II.

———•———

Many Code Talkers were not aware of the significance of their contributions. Individuals stated during interviews that they were just doing their jobs. By 2014, the number of tribes providing proof that their members served as Code Talkers rose to a total of thirty-three. Finally, in the twenty-first century, the majority of these code-talking groups are receiving recognition for their honorable service. It has taken more than sixty years to fully acknowledge these men for their achievements.

Before Comanche elder Charles Chibitty died in 2005, he participated in an interview with Sierra S. Adare for a magazine article and described how he was honored for his service. The writer asked: "The Navajos have a medal for the part they played in the war. Was there a similar medal awarded to the Comanches?" "No," Chibitty replied. "I was making a speech one time and they kept calling me a code talker. After I made the speech, there was a man there who said he knew I was a code talker but that I did not have a medal. So he pinned his medal on me. He was one of the Navajo code talkers from the Pacific. They never made one for the Comanches that were in Europe. Of course, I have an Army Good Conduct Medal . . . My tribe gave me an officer's cavalry sword, though. It is equal to the Medal of Honor among the Comanches. When we were still fighting the US Cavalry a long time ago, whoever was the top man got the saber, and now I have it."

Military medals were awarded to individuals for their gallant service to their country. Sgt. Guy Rondell, a Lakota Code Talker, received a Bronze Star for heroic action against the Japanese during World War II. Philip "Stoney" LaBlanc, also a Lakota Code Talker, received a Purple Heart for wounds received in World War II.

The French Government honored the Comanche and Choctaw Code Talkers of World Wars I and II on November 3, 1989. Their service was recognized with a special award called the Knights of the Order of National Merit, a certificate, and a plaque. As French army major Jacques de Vasselot, a liaison officer, stated during the award ceremony, "It is important to remember who helped us to be free."

South Dakota's governor, Walter D. Miller, recognized the Lakota Code Talkers of World War II in a public ceremony on September 4, 1994, which was declared Lakota Code Talker Recognition Day. Each family received a plaque. The inscription on John Bear King's read:

John Bear King
World War II
Survivor of Sioux Indian Code Talkers
302nd Reconnaissance Team
First Cavalry in the South Pacific

In addition, a memorial with seven statues representing all Native soldiers, including Indian Code Talkers, was dedicated in Pierre, South Dakota, on September 15, 2001. Many Indian veterans attended this special dedication.

The Navajo Code Talkers were awarded a top United States award on July 26, 2001. Pres. George W. Bush presented the Congressional Gold Medal to the original twenty-nine Navajo Code Talkers for their commendable service. The president stated:

> American Indians have served with the modesty and strength and quiet valor their tradition has always inspired. That tradition found full expression in the code talkers, in those absent, and in those with us today. . . . Gentlemen, your service inspires the respect and admiration of Americans, and our gratitude is expressed for all time in the medals it is now my honor to present.

The remaining Navajo Code Talkers were awarded Congressional Silver Medals during a ceremony held on November 24, 2002. The United States Representative from New Mexico, Tom Udall, spoke during the ceremony: "Their contribution to the preservation of liberty and freedom during World War II will never be forgotten and can never be diminished. . . . Let this day be another ceremony in your life in which we as a country and government recognize your achievements and rightfully give you a place in our nation's history." All in all, a total of 420 medals were presented to the Navajos.

In 2004, a hearing before the Committee on Indian Affairs took place in Washington, DC, where my friends Dr. William C. Meadows (Kiowa), Cmdr. Donald Loudner (Hunkpati Dakota), and Robin Roberts (Meskwaki) spoke to a committee that included Sen. Ben Nighthorse Campbell, Sen. John McCain, and other high-ranking officials. The testimonies provided detailed evidence about the service of Code Talkers from at least seventeen tribes in addition to the Navajo. The year ended, but Congress did not pass the bill to honor these Code Talkers.

I had the opportunity to participate in Senate meetings in Washington, DC with members of the Choctaw and Comanche tribes in 2006. My mother and I traveled with Cmdr. Don Loudner as representatives of the Sioux tribe. We joined Chief Gregory Pyle and his group, which included members from the Choctaw Nation, as well as Chairman Wallace Coffey and his colleagues from the Comanche Nation. We met with a variety of senators of the 109th Congress to gather support for bill S. 1035, the Code Talkers Recognition Act.

Also in 2006, the House of Representatives introduced a similar bill—H.R. 4597, also titled the Code Talker Recognition Act. Although these bills did not receive opposition, it took another two years for them to gain momentum and pass in Congress. In 2008, two-thirds of the Senate and the House of Representatives passed a new bill, H.R. 4544, titled the Code Talker Recognition Act of 2008. It passed into law (Public Law 110-420) and was signed by Pres. George W. Bush on October 15, 2008. President Bush had presented Congressional Medals to the surviving Navajo Code Talkers in 2001 and 2002. By signing this bill in 2008, he paved the way for each and every Code Talker who served in the United States military during World War I and World War II to be recipients of a significant honor.

Next came the task of coordinating the first strike of the medals for each tribe. Liaisons gathered and discussed ideas for each medal's design. Illustrations on the front showed men code talking on telephones, in pairs, or as individuals, and the backs had various Native American symbols, such as a tipi, buffalo,

Three tribes work together and attend Senate meetings to gain support for the Code Talker Recognition Act. Sitting left to right: Andrea Page, Mary Monsees, Bertram Bobb, and Judy Allen. Standing left to right: Allan Lovesee, Fred Bobb, Don Loudner, Chairman Wallace Coffey, Chief Gregory Pyle, Lanny Asepermy, and John Jackson. (Courtesy Andrea Page)

A visit to the US Mint in 2013. Sitting: Don Loudner. Standing left to right: Claude Black Cloud, Betty Birdsong, Andrea Page, and William Norton. (Courtesy Andrea Page)

bow and arrow, arrowhead, peace pipe, or eagle. Each tribe collaborated with Betty Birdsong, program manager in the Office of Design at the United States Mint, who stated, "Working with each tribe was a uniquely amazing experience. It gave me and the entire United States Mint a greater perspective of the different tribes' histories, and the collaborations resulted in amazing designs that will live on to help tell the history of the code talkers and the culture of each individual tribe."

After years of hard work, on November 20, 2013, Congressional Gold Medals were presented to thirty-three tribes in Washington, DC at an invitation-only ceremony in Emancipation Hall. An additional Congressional Silver Medal ceremony was held at the National Museum of the American Indian on the same day. Nearly one thousand family members of the code talkers attended the ceremonies.

Congressional Silver Medal ceremony, 2013. Left to right: Robin Roberts, Andrea Page, Don Loudner, and William C. Meadows. (Courtesy William C. Meadows)

Atrium at the National Museum of the American Indian, where the Silver Medal ceremony was held. (Courtesy Alana Page)

Just before 11:00 a.m., the Marine Corp Band began to play. Soft tunes lead into bold patriotic songs as the Gold Medal ceremony's starting time neared. A booming voice spoke from above, announcing the flag color guard, which began the ceremony. A clergy member opened with a prayer, then a number of speakers explained what the Code Talkers accomplished in the wars. One by one, they told stories of bravery, secrecy, and service above and beyond the call of duty. Each one explained the purpose of the code-talking missions: to save American lives and protect American soil, or Mother Earth. As Sen. Harry Reid said, "Despite the atrocities and struggles, the resilient Native people still answered the call to defend this country because it was home."

The Congressional Gold Medals were laid out on tables in the front of the room. I was in awe while the tribes were announced alphabetically and each tribal chairman (or representative) stood to accept their medal. Not one sound was heard in the entire space. No one spoke, cried out, or shouted congratulations. In the auditorium of invited guests plus hundreds of journalists, photographers, cameramen, and security, no one said a word. Even after the last tribe was announced, it must have been a full minute before the first clap occurred and avalanched into a full room of applause, cheering, and whooping.

Chairman Wallace Coffey and Chief Gregory Pyle at the Gold Medal ceremony. (Courtesy Andrea Page)

Don Loudner and Andrea Page at the Congressional Gold Medal ceremony, 2013. (Courtesy Andrea Page)

The Page family with Chairman Coffey at the Gold Medal ceremony at Emancipation Hall. Left to right: Jim Page, Alexa Page, Chairman Wallace Coffey, Alana Page, and Andrea Page. (Courtesy Andrea Page)

Claude Black Cloud, nephew of John Bear King, with Frank White Bull, grandson of George Sleeps From Home, after the Gold Medal ceremony. (Courtesy Andrea Page)

Code Talker Walter C. John. (Courtesy John family)

The "Walter Cody John Honor Guard" at the Congressional Silver Medal ceremony. (Courtesy John family)

At one point during the ceremonies throughout the day, Michael John, son of Code Talker Walter C. John, walked to the podium to explain what this honor meant to him. "When I was young, I was told that Indians didn't do anything. America really doesn't know what Indians did or what my father did for our country. But now I can show them this medal. We are not invisible anymore."

Sen. John Thune of South Dakota said, "So many of us in South Dakota didn't realize the story of the Code Talkers. We never knew. It's an honor for me to participate in the ceremonies today." Senator Thune introduced the first Code Talker Recognition Act in November 2001. He and fellow South Dakota senator Tim Johnson were instrumental in sponsoring multiple bills until the Code Talker Recognition Act of 2008 was finally passed.

Rosie Rios, assistant treasurer of the US Mint, knew how monumental the day's ceremonies truly were. "After four years at the US Mint, today is one of my proudest days," she said. "American Indians answered the call and displayed qualities of strength, honor, pride, devotion, and wisdom. Even though all of the Code Talkers are gone, their warrior spirits live on."

South Dakota representative Kristi Noem discussed South Dakota Code Talker Clarence Wolfguts and his testimony before a Senate committee. She repeated what Mr. Wolfguts said at that congressional hearing: "I am a full-blood Indian, and we do whatever we can to protect the United States because we love America. Nobody can ever take that away from us."

Representative Noem paused and continued in her own words, "It may have taken a while for us to get to this point, but the bravery, selflessness, and patriotism of South Dakota's Code Talkers will never be forgotten."

American Indian Code Talkers, humble and silent for a very long time, maintained their identity and culture throughout the struggles of the last century. They have shown focus, fortitude, and forgiveness, putting grudges aside so they could answer the call to protect Mother Earth. And now they have been justly honored by the government that was their enemy—and then an ally in the fight for freedom.

The wait is over, and the secret is finally out.

Appendix

Sioux Code Talkers of the 302nd Reconnaissance Troop

The Code Talkers of the 302nd Reconnaissance Troop served in New Guinea, the Admiralties, and the Philippines under Gen. Innis Palmer Swift and Gen. Douglas MacArthur. Details about the lives and service of these men have in many cases been lost to the historical record. The following has been compiled from the most complete information available.

John Bear King

Born: August 13, 1911
Died: September 2, 1949
Parents: Eugene and Rose (Edgar) Bear King
Standing Rock Sioux Tribe (Lakota)
Married: Mabel (Halsey) Bear King
Children: One son, two daughters
Occupation: Rancher
Enlisted and Served: May 18, 1943–May 14, 1945
Rank: Private First Class
Medals Awarded: Philippine Liberation Medal, World War II Victory Medal, Asiatic-Pacific Campaign Medal
After the War: Suffered from malaria and a spinal injury as a result of his service. Talented calf-roper and bronc rider; competed in local rodeos and was often in the winner's circle. Worked in the stockyard in Mobridge, South Dakota.

Edward Armstrong Eagle Boy

Born: April 2, 1918
Died: April 19, 1978
Parents: Amos and Bertha (Thielen) Eagle Boy
Cheyenne River Sioux Tribe (Lakota)
Married: Vera (Red Owl) Eagle Boy
Children: One son
Occupation: Truck driver
Enlisted and Served: Left March 31, 1942
Rank: Sergeant
Medals Awarded: Philippine Liberation Medal, World War II Victory Medal,
    Asiatic-Pacific Campaign Medal
After the War: Married his high-school sweetheart and settled in Mason City,
    Iowa.

Walter "Cody" John

Born: February 4, 1920
Died: December 24, 1998
Parents: Charles and Esther (Wolf) John
Santee Sioux Tribe (Dakota)
Married: Myrtle Lucy (Red Wing) John, then Esther (Hensley) John
Children: Four sons, then three daughters
Occupation: Worked in a beef-packing house
Enlisted and Served: Enlisted October 15, 1941
Rank: Private First Class
Medals Awarded: American Defense Service Medal, American Service Medal,
    Philippine Liberation Medal with two Bronze Service Stars, World War
    II Victory Medal, Good Conduct Medal, Asiatic-Pacifc Campaign Medal
After the War: The tribe honored his service by naming a veterans post after
    him.

Philip "Stoney" LaBlanc

Born: February 10, 1913
Died: January 17, 1998
Parents: Oliver and Josephine (Sees the Horses) LaBlanc
Cheyenne River Sioux Tribe (Minneconjou Lakota)
Married: Evangeline "Alma" (Swimmer) LaBlanc
Children: Unknown
Occupation: Unknown
Enlisted and Served: September 22, 1942–March 7, 1946
Rank: Private First Class
Medals Awarded: Purple Heart, four Bronze Battle Stars, four Major Campaign Medals, Honorable Service Lapel Button, Asiatic-Pacific Campaign Medal, Philippine Liberation Medal, World War II Victory Medal, Bronze Service Arrowhead
After the War: Unknown

Baptiste Pumpkin Seed

Born: March 2, 1923
Died: May 4, 2001
Parents: William and Lizzie (Garnier) Pumpkin Seed
Pine Ridge Sioux Tribe (Oglala Lakota)
Married: Unknown
Children: Unknown
Occupation: Unknown
Enlisted and Served: July 2, 1942–October 23, 1945
Rank: Private First Class
Medals Awarded: Philippine Liberation Medal, World War II Victory Medal, Asiatic-Pacific Campaign Medal
After the war: Buried in Holy Cross Cemetery, Pine Ridge, South Dakota.

Guy Rondell

Born: August 30, 1919
Died: July 5, 1990
Parents: Winfield and Eunice (Eagle) Rondell
Sisseton Wahpeton Sioux Tribe
Married: Harriet Margaret Rondell
Children: One son
Occupation: Pastor
Enlisted and Served: September 18, 1940–July 21, 1945
Rank: Sergeant (Rondell was also an Alamo Scout)
Medals Awarded: Silver Star, Asiatic-Pacific Campaign Medal, Philippine Liberation Medal, two Bronze Stars, American Defense Service Medal, four Overseas Service Bars
After the War: Served thirty-two years as a Presbyterian minister on the Pine Ridge Reservation.

Edmund St. John

Born: September 9, 1920
Died: October 7, 1996
Parents: Benjamin and Susan (Smells the Earth) St. John
Crow Creek Sioux Tribe
Married: Mildred (Rabbit) St. John
Children: Unknown number of children and stepchildren
Occupation: Farmer
Enlisted and Served: June 5, 1941–December 27, 1945
Rank: Private First Class
Medals Awarded: Four Bronze Stars, two Bronze Arrowheads, Good Combat Medal, Purple Heart, Asiatic-Pacific Campaign Medal, Philippine Liberation Medal, World War II Victory Medal
After the War: Worked as a farmer and helped others when needed.

Bibliography

Books, Magazine Articles, Newspaper Articles, Brochures, and Journal Articles

Ablonka, Marc Phillip. "The Unbreakable Code." *National Amvet* Fall 1999: 9-11. Web.

Adare, Sierra S. "The Last Comanche Code Talker." *World War II* Jan. 2002: 58-64. Web.

Bernstein, Alison R. *American Indians and World War II: Toward a New Era in Indian Affairs*. Norman: University of Oklahoma Press, 1991. Print.

Boudreau, Wm. H. "Indian Code Talkers." *The SABER* (Copperas Cove, Texas) 1999, March/April ed.: 8. Print.

Cannon, M. Hamlin. *Leyte: The Return to the Philippines*. Washington, DC: Center of Military History, United States Army, 1993. Print.

Cash, Joseph H. and Herbert T. Hoover. *To Be an Indian: An Oral History*. New York: Holt, Rinehart, and Winston, 1971. 64. Print.

Contey-Aiello, Rose. *The 50th Anniversary Commemorative Album of the Flying Column, 1945-1995: The Liberation of Santo Tomas Internment Camp, February 3, 1945*. Palm Harbor, FL: R. Contey-Aiello, 1994. Print.

Davidson, Martha. "Secret Warriors." *National Museum of the American Indian* Spring 2002: 15-20. Web.

Dunn, Si. *The 1st Cavalry Division: A Historical Overview, 1921-1983*. Dallas, TX: Taylor Publishing, 1984. Print.

Elk, Black and John Gneisenau Neihardt. *Black Elk Speaks: Being the Life Story of a Holy Man of the Oglala Sioux*. Lincoln: University of Nebraska, 1995. Print.

Franco, Jere' Bishop. *Crossing the Pond: The Native American Effort in World War II*. Denton, TX: University of North Texas Press, 1999. Print.

Hat, Albert White, and Jael Kampfe. *Reading and Writing the Lakota Language (Lakota Iyapi Un Wowapi Nahan Yawapi)*. Salt Lake City: University of Utah Press, 1999. 28-29. Print.

Indians at Work May/June (1943): n.p. Print.

Indians in the War. November ed. Chicago, IL: U.S. Department of the Interior, Office of Indian Affairs, 1945. Print.

Introduction to Indian Nations in the United States, An. Washington, DC: National Congress of American Indians, n.d. 4-6. Print.

"Invasion Planning, The Battle for Los Negros Beachhead, Final Mopping Up on Manus." *The Admiralties: Operations of the 1st Cavalry Division 29 February-18 May 1944.* Comp. War Department, Historical Division. Washington, DC: Center of Military History United States Army, 1945/1990. 4+. Print. American Forces In Action.

Langan, John Gibbons. "Soon-to-be Soldier Hitchhikes His Way through Wyoming in 1941." *Casper-Star Tribune: The Wyoming History Traveler* (Casper, Wyoming) 1991: n.p. Print. Copy provided by Jack Langan.

Latza, Greg. *Blue Stars: A Selection of Stories From South Dakota's World War II Veterans.* Sioux Falls, SD: PeopleScapes, 2004. Print.

Little Eagle, Avis. "Lakota Code Talker Recalls World War II Service." *Aberdeen American News* 9 June 1994: 5A. Print.

Little Eagle, Avis. "World War II Lakota Code Talkers Used Language to Outwit the Enemy." *Indian Country Today (The Lakota Times)* 8 June 1994, Regional sec.: B3. Print.

Little Eagle, Avis. "World War II Warriors: Proud Showing for American Indian Vets at World War II Memorial Dedication." *Lakota Journal* 2-8 Nov. 2001: C2-C3. Print.

Looks for Buffalo Hand, Floyd. *Learning Journey on the Red Road.* Ed. Marc Alexander Huminilowycz. Toronto: Learning Journey Communications, 1998. 41-42. Print.

Marshall, Joseph. *Returning to the Lakota Way: Old Values to Save a Modern World.* Carlsbad, CA: Hay House, 2013. Print.

McCoy, Michael, and Jean-Marie Heskett. *Through My Mother's Eyes: The Story of a Young Girl's Life as a Prisoner of War in the Santo Tomas Internment Camp.* New York, NY: Strategic Book, 2008. Print.

McGraw, Ralph C. and Frank R. Bent. "We Were First In Manila." *The Cavalry Journal* LIV. July/August (1945): 2-3. Web. 2015.

Meadows, William C. *The Comanche Code Talkers of World War II.* Austin: University of Texas Press, 2002. Print.

Miller, John. *MacArthur and the Admiralties.* Washington, DC: Center of Military History, US Army, 1990. Print.

Morrison, Joan. "Pastor Rondell Recalls Philippine Liberation." *The Gordon (Nebraska) Journal* n.d.: n.p. Print. Copy sent from Aloma McGaa.

Potter, Dottie. "Memories and Lives of WWII Veterans." *Lakota Journal* 3-9 Sept. 2001: B5. Print.

Potter, Dottie. "The Sioux Were the First 'Code Talkers.'" *Lakota Journal* (Rapid City, SD) 8-15 Nov. 2002: A6-A7. Print.

"Powwow 134th Annual Homecoming Celebration." *Indian Country Today* (Rapid City, SD) 5 July 2000, Lakota Times sec.: D3. Print

Report of the 1st Cavalry Division, comp. "1st Cavalry Division in the Leyte Campaign." *The Cavalry Journal* LIV. November/December (1945): 2-5. Web. 2015.

Ricker, Eli S., and Richard E. Jensen. *Voices of the American West, Volume 1: The Indian Interviews of Eli S. Ricker, 1903-1919.* Lincoln: University of Nebraska Press, 2005. Print.

Rodgers, Michael. *Indian Code-Talkers of WWII.* n.d.: n.p. Print. Email copy sent from Aloma McGaa.

Rose, Stuart. "Eyes, Ears, and Nose of the Army." *The Cavalry Journal* LII. March/April (1943): 64-65. Web. 2015.

Shaffer, Mark. "Forgotten Heroes." *The Arizona Republic* 6 Jan. 2001: A1+. Print.

Sheldon, Charles A. "Cavalry's First Team in Japan." *The Armored Cavalry Journal* LV. November/December (1946): 2-3. Web. 2015.

Shields, Kenny. "Walking in Balance: A Gift from God." *Wotanin Wowapi* (Poplar, MT) 17 Mar. 2005: 4A. Print.

"Sioux Observer and Receiver Make Things Easy for Gunner." *The Stars and Stripes* 10 Jan. 1919. Print.

Smith, Robert Ross. *The War in the Pacific: Triumph in the Philippines.* Washington, DC: Center of Military History, US Army, 1991. Print.

Stanton, Shelby L. *Order of Battle, U.S. Army, World War II.* NY: Presido Press, 1984. 71. Print.

Steward, Hal D. "First Cavalry Division." *The Armored Cavalry Journal* LV. November/December (1946): 5-6. Web. 2015.

St. John, Lt. Joseph and Howard Handleman. *Leyte Calling.* New York: Vanguard, 1945. Print.

"The World Is Their Warpath." *YANK The Army Newspaper* 26 Aug. 1942: 18. Print.

Waln, Vi. "Family of Lakota Code Talker Receives World War II Service Medals." *Lakota Journal* (Rapid City, SD) 12-19 Dec. 2003: B2. Print.

"World War II Memorial." *Lakota Journal* (Rapid City, SD) 13-19 Aug. 2001: B3. Print.

Wright, Bertram C. *History of The 1st Cavalry Division in World War II.* Tokyo: Toppan Printing, 1947. Print.

Interviews, Letters, and Emails

Ashley, Janna (and Vernon). "Meeting with Congressman John Thune about Sioux Code Talkers Recognition Act." 7 Nov. 2001. E-mail.

Bentley, Donald. Telephone interview. 28 Nov. 1995.

Boudreau, Wm. Harry. "First Cavalry Association Historian." 5 Sept. 1999. E-mail.

Bradley, John H. "Raiding Ground Forces in SW Pacific." Letter to Donald H. Walton. 21 Apr. 1998. MS. Houston, Texas.

Bright, Patricia S. (Osage). Telephone interview. 31 Jul. 1996.

Brooke, Mary J. (Archives Technician, National Archives). Telephone interview. 1997.

"Code Talker Exhibit, Nimitz Museum." Telephone interview. 1996.

Daily, Edward. "Army/ Cavalry Vocabulary Q & A." 2 Jan. 2000. E-mail.

Dallaston, Gayle. "Camp Strathpine 4 Jan. 2000. E-mail.

Dohr, George. "302nd Reconnaissance Troop." Interview. June 2004.

Dorfman, Merlin. E-mail interview. 11 Sept. 1995.

Draper, Steven. "First Cavalry Division." Telephone interview. 1999.

Dreighton, Lee. "Camp Strathpine." Message to the author. 16 Aug. 2001. E-mail.

Dunn, Si. Telephone interview. 23 Aug. 1998.

Edmunds, John W. "Military Records Inquiry." Interview. June 1994.

Edmunds, John W. Telephone interview. 31 July 1996.

Hawkins, Jeri (daughter of John Bear King). Telephone interview. 16 Nov. 1995.

Hawkins, Mabel. Telephone interview. 16 Nov. 1995.

Ingram, Ronald. Telephone interview. Jan. 2000.

John, Michael, Sr. "Information about Second John." Telephone interview. 3 Sept. 2001.

John, Michael, Sr. "Native American recognition." Telephone interview. 20 Dec. 2013.

Junot, Gen. Arthur. Telephone interview. 13 Aug. 1997.

Krile, Katherine. "Hopi Code Talkers." Message to the author. 8 July 2005. E-mail.

LaBlanc, Philip and Alma. Telephone interview. 20 Nov. 1995.

LaBlanc, Philip (Stoney), Lakota Code Talker. Telephone interview. 30 Jul. 1996.

Langan, John Gibbons. Letters to author. 1996-2002. MS. Jackson Hole, WY.

Langan, John Gibbons. Interview. June 1996.

Langan, John Gibbons. "Responding to Call for Information." Letter to author. 12 Nov. 1996. MS. Jackson Hole, WY.

Langan, John (Jack) Gibbons. "Coded Words." Letter to author. 6 May 2000. MS. Jackson, WY.

LeBeau, Marcella. Telephone interviews. 16 Nov. 1995-present.

Little Eagle, Avis. Telephone interview. 1994.

McDonald, Helen. Telephone interview. 1996.

Meadows, William C. Telephone interviews. 4 Aug. 1999-present.

"Oyate Iyechinka Woglakapi: An Oral History Collection." Interview. *American Indian Research Project: South Dakota Oral History Center, University of South Dakota, Vemillion* 1970-1979: n.p. Print.

Red Boy, Shirley Quinton. Telephone interview. 29 Sept. 2005.

Red Boy, Shirley Quinton. Telephone interview. 3 Jan. 2000.

Red Boy, Shirley Quinton. Telephone interview. 4 Oct. 2004.

Red Elk, Lenora and Shields, Kenny. Telephone interview. 30 July 1996.

Red Elk, Lenora. Telephone interview. 14 Mar. 1997.

Red Elk, Priscilla. Telephone interview. 2005.

Roberts, Robin (Meskwaki). Telephone interview. 5 Oct. 2004.

Rondell, Mr. (brother of Guy Rondell). Telephone interview. 1999.

Shupla, Franklin (Hopi). Telephone interview. 1999.

Songey, Alfred. Telephone interview. 2000.

Vasquez, Henry. Telephone interview. Aug. 2005.

Vasquez, Manuel. Telephone interview. 19 Aug. 2005.

Walton, Ret. Col. Donald H. "302nd Address List." Letter to author. 22 May 2000. MS. Walton Distributing Co., Inc., San Antonio, Texas.

Walton, Ret. Col. Donald H. "Lakota Code Talkers and Platoon Leaders." Letter to author. 18 May 2000. MS. San Antonio, Texas.

Walton, Ret. Col. Donald H. Letters to author. 1997-2000. MS. San Antonio, Texas.

Walton, Ret. Col. Donald H. Interview. Aug. 1998.

Walton, Ret. Col. Donald H. "Q&A First Cavalry Division." Letter to author. 12 Nov. 1997. MS. San Antonio, Texas.

Westover, Delores (daughter of John Bear King). Telephone interview. 20 Oct. 2001.

Wydler, Dara. "Flying Column question." 12 Oct. 2016. E-mail.

"Yanktonai." E-mail interview. 23 Feb. 1995.

Historical Reports, Discharge Papers, and Government Publications

302nd Operational Records. College Park, MD: National Archives, n.d. Print.

302nd Rcn Trp Historical Report (Admiralty). Rep. no. 901-CAV-0.3 8070. College Park, MD: National Archives, n.d. Print. 9 Mar-18 May 1944.

302nd Rcn Trp Historical Report (Luzon). Rep. n.p.: n.d. Print. Item 2472 Reel 2234. Copy provided by Ret. Col. Donald Walton.

41st Infantry Division Unit History 1944, 163rd Infantry Regiment. Rep. no. 341-INF (163)- 0.1. College Park, MD: National Archives. Print.

CG 2nd Brigade and CG US Forces, trans. *War Department Historical Record Declassified Document (901-0.12) (7575).* 1944. 1st Cav Div- Admiralty (Brewer) Islands Campaign- In Messages File 26 Feb-18 May 1944. National Archives, College Park, MD.

Daily Radio File Brewer OPN. Rep. no. 901-2.4 / 7581. 10 Mar-18 May 44 ed. College Park, MD: National Archives, 1996. Print. Box 16408 270/60/24/6.

Gardner, Hugh, Capt. Inf., comp. *National Archives Declassified Document (901-0.1).* 1 Jan. 1945. The History of the 1st Cavalry Division. National Archives, June 2000, College Park, MD.

Historical Report-Brewer. Rep. no. 901-CAV-0.3 / 8070. 9 Mar-18 May 44 ed. College Park, MD: National Archives, 1996. Print. Box 16469 270/60/26/1.

Historical Report-Leyte Campaign. Rep. no. 901-CAV-0.3 / 48671. 6 Oct 44-8 Jan 45 ed. College Park, MD: National Archives, 1996. Print. Box 16469 270/60/26/1.

Historical Report-Luzon Campaign. Rep. no. 901-CAV-0.3. 21 Jan-Jun 45 ed. College Park, MD: National Archives, 1997. Print. Box 16469 270/60/26/1.

Membership Directory. Rep. no. 901-1.7. 17 Jul 44-47 ed. College Park, MD: National Archives, 1996. Print. Box 16397 270/60/24/4.

Milich, Leo, 1st Lt. Cav. *War Department Historical Record Declassified Document (901-CAV-0.3).* 1944. 302nd Cav Rcn Troop Historical Report Admiralty (Brewer) Island Campaign 9 Mar-18 May 1944. National Archives, College Park, MD.

Swift, Innis, Gen., comp. *National Archives Declassified Document (901-2.4) (7581).* 2 Apr. 1944. G-2 Daily Radio Summary File- 1st Cav Div 10 Mar-18 May 44. National Archives, 1996, College Park, MD.

Unit History. Rep. no. 901-CAV. Dec 43-9 Mar 44 ed. College Park, MD: National Archives, 1997. Print. Box 16469.

Unit History. Rep. no. 901-CAV. Jun-Dec 45 ed. College Park, MD: National Archives, 1997. Print. Box 16469.

United States. United States Senate. Committee on Indian Affairs. *Hearing Before the Committee on Indian Affairs.* September 22, 2004 ed. Washington, DC: US Government Printing Office, 2004. Print. Second Session on Contributions of Native American Code Talkers in American Military History.

Walton, Ret. Col. Donald H. *Recollections of the Trip to Manila.* n.d. n.p.

Websites and Videos

"Brief History Wounded Knee Massacre December 29, 1890." University of Montana, n.d. Web. 15 Oct. 2005.

"Code Talker Recognition Act." *H.R.4544—Code Talkers Recognition Act of 2008*. Ed. Dan Boren. Congress.gov, n.d. Web. 23 Nov. 2014. <https://www.congress.gov/bill/110th-congress/house-bill/4544>.

Cordero, John, Gunnery Sgt. "Marine Corps Logistics Base Barstow." *WWII Navajo Code Talkers Receive Silver Medal News Article Display*. Marines: Official Website of the United States Marine Corps, 24 Nov. 2001. Web. 4 July 2013. <http://www.mclbbarstow.marines.mil/News/NewsArticleDisplay/tabid/9411/Article/508996/wwii-navajo-code-talkers-receive-silver-medal.aspx>.

"First Cavalry Division WWII Manila Stock Footage and Images." *First Cavalry Division WWII Manila Historical Stock Footage and Video. 5525 First Cavalry Division WWII Manila Royalty Free Video Clips and Pictures Available for Download*. Critical Past, n.d. Web. 27 May 2013.

"Guy Rondell, SWST Codetalker." *Sota Iya Ye Yapi*. News of the Lake Traverse Reservation, n.d. Web. 17 Jan. 2004.

Kent, Jim. "Anniversary of the Return of the Ghost Dance Shirt." *Dakota Digest*. South Dakota Public Broadcasting, n.d. Web. 5 July 2013. <http://www.sdpb.sd.gov/newsite/shows.aspx?MediaID=39544&Parmtype=RADIO&ParmAccessLevel=sdpb-all>.

"Liberation of POWs in the Philippines." *YouTube*. BCMFofNM, n.d. Web. 30 May 2012.

Little Elk, David. "Medicine Wheel and 7 Lakota Virtues." *Medicine Wheel*. Malakota.com, n.d. Web. 27 May 2004.

"Oceti-Sakowin." *South Dakota Public Broadcasting*. South Dakota Documentaries, n.d. Web. 23 Mar. 2013.

"Oyate FAQs." *Oyate—FAQs—Frequently Asked Questions*. Oyate, n.d. Web. 29 Mar. 2005.

Parker, Mrs. Z. A. "Ghost Dance - Lakota Ghost Dance at Pine Ridge Reservation, June 20, 1890." *Ghost Dance - Lakota Ghost Dance at Pine Ridge Reservation, June 20, 1890*. n.p., n.d. Web. 5 July 2013. <http://www.ghostdance.com/history/history-zaparker.html>. Text originally from James Mooney, The Ghost-dance Religion and the Sioux Outbreak of 1890, 14th Annual Report of the Bureau of American Ethnology, Part 2 (1894).

Pollard, Liz. "Petition for Code Talker Medals." *Moccasin Telegraph, Tribal News*. n.p., n.d. Web. 2 Jan. 2000.

"Santo Tomas Internment Camp." *Santo Tomas Internment Camp.* n.p., n.d. Web. 30 May 2012.

"Santo Tomas Prisoners Liberated; FDR on Yalta 1945/3/1." *YouTube.* Universal Newsreels, n.d. Web. 30 May 2012.

"Secrets of Santo Tomas (Five Women are Executed) Rainer Loeser." *YouTube.* Unitedmovietone, n.d. Web. 30 May 2012.

Smith, Bill. "World War 2 Lost Evidence—Leyte Gulf—Part 2." *YouTube.* YouTube, n.d. Web. 23 Mar. 2013.

"Through My Mother's Eyes." *YouTube.* Doc McCoy, n.d. Web. 30 May 2012.

"Turtle Island Storyteller Marcella LeBeau." *Wisdom of the Elders.* Wisdom of the Elders.org, n.d. Web. 5 July 2013. <http://wisdomoftheelders.org/turtle-island-storyteller-marcella-lebeau/>.

"University of Santo Tomas during the 2nd World War." *YouTube.* Michael Reyes, 27 Jan. 2010. Web. 30 May 2012.

Waldrip, Olen E. *1st Cavalry Division, 7th Cavalry Regiment.* July 1943. VHS Video. Ft. Hood, Texas.

White Hat, Albert, Sr. "Lakota Health & Culture (Fall 2012)." *YouTube.* Sintegleskautube, 7 Sept. 2012. Web. 2015.

Zielinski, Michael. "Lakota Standing Rock Sioux Tribe Congressional Gold Medal Designs." *Daily Coin Collecting News.* Coin Update, 9 Jul. 2012. Web. 4 July 2013. <http://news.coinupdate.com/lakota-standing-rock-sioux-tribe-congressional-gold-medal-designs-1731/>.

Index

Teacher's Guide

Common Core Standards

Reading/Literacy Standards
Key Ideas and Details

CCSS.ELA-LITERACY.RL.6-8.1
Cite textual evidence to support analysis of what the text says explicitly as well as inferences drawn from the text.

CCSS.ELA-LITERACY.RL.6-8.2
Determine a theme or central idea of a text and how it is conveyed through particular details; provide a summary of the text distinct from personal opinions or judgments.

Craft and Structure

CCSS.ELA-LITERACY.RL.6-8.4
Determine the meaning of words and phrases as they are used in a text, including figurative, connotative, and technical meanings.

CCSS.ELA-LITERACY.RI.6-8.6
Determine an author's point of view or purpose in a text and explain how it is conveyed in the text.

Integration of Knowledge and Ideas

CCSS.ELA-LITERACY.RI.6-8.7
Integrate information presented in different media or formats (e.g., visually, quantitatively) as well as in words to develop a coherent understanding of a topic or issue.

CCSS.ELA-LITERACY.RH.6-8.8
Distinguish among fact, opinion, and reasoned judgment in a text.

Writing Standards
CCSS.ELA-LITERACY.W.6-8.7
Conduct short research projects to answer a question, drawing on several sources and refocusing the inquiry when appropriate.

CCSS.ELA-LITERACY.W.6-8.10
Write routinely over extended time frames (time for research, reflection, and revision) and shorter time frames (a single sitting or a day or two) for a range of discipline-specific tasks, purposes, and audiences.

Social Studies Framework and Practices
CCSS.SS.A.7-8 Gathering, Interpreting and Using Evidence
1. Define and frame questions about the United States that can be answered by gathering, interpreting, and using evidence.
4. Describe and analyze arguments of others, with support.

CCSS.SS.B.7-8 Chronological Reasoning
1. Identify how events are related chronologically to one another in time and explain the ways in which earlier ideas and events may influence subsequent ideas and events.
3. Identify causes and effects, using examples from current events, grade-level content, and historical events.

CCSS.SS.C.7-8 Comparison and Contextualization
2. Identify and categorize multiple perspectives on a given historical experience.

CCSS.SS.D.7-8 Geographic Reasoning
1. Use location terms and geographic representations such as maps, photographs, satellite images, and models to describe where places in early United States history were in relation to each other.
3. Identify and analyze how environments affect human activities and how human activities affect physical environments in the United States.

CCSS.SS.F.7-8 Civic Participation
1. Demonstrate respect for the rights of others in discussions.

CCSS.SS.7.1 Native Americans
The physical environment and natural resources of North America influenced the development of the first human settlements and the culture of Native Americans. Native American societies [vary] across North America.

CCSS.SS.7.6 Westward Expansion
Driven by political and economic motives, the United States expanded its physical boundaries to the Pacific Ocean between 1800 and 1860. This settlement displaced Native Americans as the frontier was pushed westward.

7.6c. Westward expansion provided opportunities for some groups while harming others.

CCSS.SS.8.6 World War II
The aggression of the Axis powers threatened United States security and led to its entry into World War II. The nature and consequences of warfare during World War II transformed the United States and the global community.

Big Idea Topics

Courage	Plains History
Bravery	Forgiveness
Survival	Leadership
Teamwork	Sacrifice

Pre-Reading Activities

Writing Prompts
Life Review . . . Your Memories . . . Making Connections

- What is your story of home? Where is your home located? What was your early childhood like? Describe a typical day in your life.
- What has made you proud of your parents?
- Describe a defining moment in your childhood.
  - Was it a peak experience where you accomplished something outstanding?
  - Was it a moment of excitement?
  - Was it a funny experience?
  - How did your point of view change because of the defining moment?
- Describe the characteristics of a great leader.

Preview . . . Building Background

- Take ten minutes to study the front cover, read the back cover and inside flaps, and the first page of chapter 1. Then flip through the rest of the book, skimming for vocabulary and glancing at the photos.
- Identify five facts about the Sioux Code Talkers of World War II.
- Brainstorm a list of ten facts you know about any of the following topics:

Sioux Indians
The Great Plains
World War II
The Cavalry
Code Talkers

- Share your list with a partner. Add to and/or edit your list.
- Locate one photo in the book. Describe what you think the photo reveals (making inferences).
- Ask a thoughtful question and set a purpose to read further. Make a prediction.
- Use photos from the book and create a Graffiti Wall for each one. Have students go on a Gallery Walk around the room to study the photos, notice details, and record facts on the wall.

Reading Activities

Vocabulary Study

- Locate unknown vocabulary in the text and brainstorm five to ten additional words that help the reader make connections and understand the word. Use the website Visuwords if needed.
- Make flash cards using index cards and/or an interactive online app like Quizlet.
- Complete a List-Group-Label activity with a partner and share with the whole group.

Vocabulary List

Chapter 1
Reminisced
Buggy
Barter
Deployed
Dense
Wrest
Lakota
Sioux
Reconnaissance
Platoon
Mission

Chapter 2
Migrating
Nomadic
Fortitude
Wisdom
Conflicts
Sustains
Prospectors
Treaty
Deteriorating

Chapter 3
Draft office
Maneuvers
Combat
Bayonet
Amphibious
Scouts
Generations
Specialized
Transmissions
Invasions

Chapter 4
Vowed
Mechanized
Perimeter
Patrolling
Dominated
Embarked
Inspect
Strategy
Trooper
Reinforcements

Chapter 5
Productive
Monitor
Inspection
Ration
Accommodations
Prisoner
Debris
Flanking
Withered
Internment camp

Chapter 6
Honorable
Discharge
Resilient
Veteran
Offensive
Observer
Coordinates
Negotiated
Recruits
Recognition

Activity

Authors Play with Words

Objectives:
- To utilize a personal list of new vocabulary words connected to *Sioux Code Talkers of World War II.*
- To demonstrate an increased understanding of the word meanings, which therefore aids in comprehension of a complex text.

Directions:
- Pre-assess a list of vocabulary words. Make a personal list of words to study.
- Before the activity, students will choose words from their personal word list to complete the left side of the Knowledge Chart (available to download from www.pelicanpub.com).
- Review how readers think about words.
- Complete an Authors Play with Words Task Card (available to download from www.pelicanpub.com) with one vocabulary word each (five words/five task cards).
- Students will use new vocabulary words in their own writing.

- After the activity, students will complete the right side of the Knowledge Chart.
- Compare both sides. Students will determine how their vocabulary improved.

Differentiation:
- Content: Teacher can limit the number of words to study.
- Process: Teacher can provide scaffolded task cards.
- Product: Teacher can provide a variety of models of writing that students can use in a digital product, like Voki, Phrase It, or Comic Creator.

How Do We Think About Words?

Read the lines from the book *Sioux Code Talkers of World War II.* The words in CAPITAL LETTERS show how a reader can think about words.

- DEFINITION (What does the word mean?)
  p. 25 "Then the cavalry *soldiers*, also known as *troopers*, receive orders to move inland."

- VISUALIZING (What actions can you see in your mind?)
  p. 24 "The men experience an *amphibious* landing: the naval ships anchor and the landing crafts take off for the beach.

- ASSOCIATIONS (Make similar connections.)
  p. 31 What word is used to describe how the buffalo move across the Plains? ***Migrating***

  p. 31 "**Migrat**ing buffalo herds extend as far as the eye can see . . ."
  Make connections to other vocabulary with similar word parts: **migrat**e, **migrat**ory, im**migrat**e.

- TONE/MOOD (How do those words make you feel?)
  p. 38 ". . . the Indian bands were *forced* to make stationary homesteads, *stripped* of their nomadic ways."
  p. 46 ". . . the same people who moved them into a *confined* space and *ordered* them not to leave."

- ANTONYMS (Words that have opposite meanings)
  p. 47 ". . . they *enlisted*, which meant they joined voluntarily . . ."
  p. 47 ". . . they were *drafted*, which meant they were required . . . to report for military duty."

- CONTEXT CLUES (How is the word used in the sentence?)
  p. 50 "They learned the basics of hand-to-hand combat with *bayonets*."

- NEW USES (Use words in creative ways, like in comparisons, analogies, etc.)
  p. 60 "The Momote Airfield *flaunted* a runway of flat, hard, well-drained coral soil."

Read, Stop, and Think

Use the Read, Stop, and Think graphic organizer worksheets (available to download from www.pelicanpub.com) to collect evidence from the book and think about what is being read.

1. What are the big ideas?
2. What are the origins of conflict?
3. What are multiple perspectives concerning an issue?

Make a Timeline

Plot some of the important historical events while you read. Use an interactive timeline website, like Dipity, ReadWriteThink, or Tiki-Toki.

Post-Reading Activities

Mini-Research

The Sioux Code Talkers traveled to many different parts of the world. Choose a place from the list below and learn more about it:

The Great Plains	Australia
Sioux Reservations	New Guinea
North and South Dakota	The Philippines
Texas	Pacific Ocean
California	Japan

Other topics for research might include:

- Native American tribes
- The First Cavalry Division
- Notable historical leaders, such as Sitting Bull and Crazy Horse, or General Custer and General MacArthur, or any of the presidents from the 1800s and 1900s.
- North American bison, or buffalo
- Military vehicles
- Your own family history story. Interview your grandfather or grandmother to uncover the best story to share.

Compare and Contrast Writing Topics

- Values of different cultures
- Leaders of different societies
- Environments and habitats on different continents
- Time periods (1800s and 1900s)

Making Connections

- Make a Top 10 List of facts you learned about code talking.
- Identify one of the Lakota values. How can you adapt and develop this value in your own life?
- If you could, which leader would you like to spend a day with? What would you do?
- How important is Mother Earth? Is Mother Earth worth protecting? How will you help?